PENGUIN BOOKS
SRI SATHYA SAI BABA

Bill Aitken is Scottish by birth, a naturalized Indian by choice. He studied comparative religion at Leeds University and then hitch-hiked to India in 1959. He has lived in Himalayan ashrams, worked as secretary to a maharani, freelanced under his middle name (Liam McKay) and undertaken miscellaneous excursions—from Nanda Devi to Sabarimala—on an old motorbike and by steam railway.

Aitken has written on travel and tourism for newspapers and magazines in India for several years and is the author of *The Nanda Devi Affair*, *Riding the Ranges* and *Branch Line to Eternity* among other books.

To
DoRis

Please read &
let me have your
Comments

FRom
Bala.

2007

Sri Sathya Sai Baba

A Life

BILL AITKEN

PENGUIN BOOKS

PENGUIN BOOKS
Published by the Penguin Group
Penguin Books India Pvt. Ltd, 11 Community Centre, Panchsheel Park, New Delhi 110 017,
India
Penguin Group (USA) Inc., 375 Hudson Street, New York, New York 10014, USA
Penguin Group (Canada), 90 Eglinton Avenue East, Suite 700, Toronto, Ontario, M4P 2Y3,
Canada (a division of Pearson Penguin Canada Inc.)
Penguin Books Ltd, 80 Strand, London WC2R 0RL, England
Penguin Ireland, 25 St Stephen's Green, Dublin 2, Ireland (a division of Penguin Books Ltd)
Penguin Group (Australia), 250 Camberwell Road, Camberwell, Victoria 3124, Australia
(a division of Pearson Australia Group Pty Ltd)
Penguin Group (NZ), cnr Airborne and Rosedale Roads, Albany, Auckland 1310, New
Zealand (a division of Pearson New Zealand Ltd)
Penguin Group (South Africa) (Pty) Ltd, 24 Sturdee Avenue, Rosebank, Johannesburg 2196,
South Africa

Penguin Books Ltd, Registered Offices: 80 Strand, London WC2R 0RL, England

First published in Viking by Penguin Books India 2004
Published in Penguin Books 2006

Copyright © Bill Aitken 2004

Photographs courtesy Keki Mistri and Sri Madan Mohan Krishna Yachendra,
Raja of Venkatagiri

10 9 8 7 6 5 4 3 2 1

ISBN-10: 0144 00061X; ISBN-13: 9780144000616

Typeset in Sabon by SÜRYA, New Delhi
Printed at Saurabh Printers Pvt. Ltd, Noida

Sharanam Ganesha: Ganesha Sharanam

Contents

Preface

*It is a long road to the feet of the One but thither do
we all travel.*

—Rudyard Kipling in *Kim*

To write about the life and times of Sri Sathya Sai
Baba is to take on a seemingly impossible task. How
does one convey his apparent divine status without inviting
either disbelief or incredulity? If written entirely for non-
believers, the story will remain half-told. Nor is it fair to
reduce well-verified facts of a seemingly miraculous nature
into a catalogue of neutral rationalizations. As the mystic-
mountaineer W.H. Murray puts it, 'The aim is not to
abrogate reason but raise it. A camel cannot pass through
the eye of a needle but vision can.' Murray advocates the
alchemical art of 'oneing' to help us cross the seemingly
unbridgeable gap between our world and the realm of the
spirit, thereby harmonizing the lessons of the head with
the teachings of the heart.

The only way an itinerant student of religion (as
opposed to a Sai devotee) can explain the Sai phenomenon

is by resorting to his traveller's diary in which, for three weeks each winter over a dozen years, he recorded the hidden wonders of the Deccan's topography and its rich theology. The author, to borrow Thomas Carlyle's comment on the poet Robert Burns, 'speaks forth what is in him not from any outward call of vanity but because his heart is too full to be silent'.

This historical and theological survey, while seeking to investigate the nimbus surrounding Sathya Sai Baba and Shirdi Sai Baba does not, for the most part, express opinions for or against the fabulous associations that have arisen around their names. What it does attempt, since serious students of the operation of grace want material they can (in Sathya Sai Baba's words) 'watch, study and weigh', is an investigation of its inscrutable source as well as the details of its working on a beneficiary who can vouch for its impact. If, on occasion, this has meant a digression into explanations of how a wandering Scot came to be enamoured of the Deccan and its line of extraordinary exemplars of spiritual grace, I apologize in advance.

I have to thank Shalini Sreenivas for suggesting that this book be written and for supplying material and encouragement to enable its completion. David Davidar at Penguin has regularly lent support to the author's offbeat interests, while to Karthika has fallen the exacting task of making sense of and adding clarity to this numinous excursion. To Himanshu Bhagat I am indebted for his cool overview of largely inscrutable terrain and to Shantanu Ray Choudhary for his invaluable remedial insights. Rajiv Mehrotra kindly helped speed the typescript on its way, aided by Lalita in Delhi and Jayashree in

Bangalore. I also need to thank Paras, our faithful and exuberant jungli dog, who enabled deadlines to be met by waking me up each morning. My main inspiration has been the boundless love Rani-ma feels for her guru, Sri Sathya Sai. To the source of that love this book is offered with reverence.

Mussoorie
April 2004

{1}

A Means to Grace

There are dozens of brands of religion, but one spirit that informs them all. Anyone who hawks the proposition that one brand is better than another implies he has tasted them all which would either make him omniscient or, more likely, a salesman seeking to pass off bluff as certainty. The student of religion learns to be wary of such claims, trusting his own experience of the spirit, no matter how modest that may be. Specially in an account of the Sai Baba phenomena, it is important to stress the significance of content over form at the outset.

Both the masters, Shirdi Sai and Sathya Sai, emphasize the need to go beyond the outer labels and taste the inner spirit. While religion mostly connotes passive public belief routinely handed down, awareness of religion's informing spirit calls for a deeper individual response to the reality of the divine. The first is taught by the indoctrination of the mind, the second experienced spontaneously by the heart. Sai Baba's following, which appears to comprise a religious movement, is actually more a moving faith in the spirit, a coming together of individuals convinced that they have a direct emotional bond with their chosen master. This experience is not confined to extra-sensitive souls (what the world calls 'mystics') but is enjoyed by ordinary people who respond to the presence of either of the two Sai Baba figures with a heart full of love.

And the essence of love is to share. When I was asked to write about the life and times of the saint, avoiding the hagiographic excesses that believers find hard not to indulge in, and which puts off the ordinary seeker who wants information not hype, I agreed to give it a try. What Sathya Sai Baba arouses in me is a feeling so maddeningly beautiful that I am convinced everyone in the world would wish to experience it. Unfortunately, Sathya Sai's healing abilities have been overlaid by the bad press that stalks all those who claim acquaintance with what is holy. Many who could be helped in their search for health and wholeness choose to trust reports in the media over the wisdom of their own instincts. This biographical essay aims to dispel the doubts of these faltering spirits.

I was initially reluctant to take up this assignment because religion in India is a touchy subject these days, especially when tackled by someone born outside the subcontinent. Also, I am unacquainted with Telugu, the native language of Sathya Sai, though of all Indian tongues I find it the most ravishing on the ear. When it was pointed out that even Sathya Sai Baba's recognized biographer, Professor Kasturi, was unfamiliar with Telugu and had, on one famous occasion, clothed a gathering of ancient rishis in modern bush shirts, I took heart. Anyway, the grace that Sathya Sai embodies can only be expressed through the language of love and that is universal.

Having penned almost a dozen travel books, it seemed to me that the muse had finally acknowledged the creak of ancient bones (and a typewriter hostile to technological innovation), so that the only option left was to journey within. The necessary inspiration (and hardware) for this came from an old student of, and now a worker for, Sai Baba, whose energy and self-confidence are so impressive they could only have originated from his shakti-centre at Puttaparthi. All my reservations and wringing of hands were overruled by the promise that Sathya Sai would somehow intervene to speed up the project. Against the inertia that old age feels it has earned, I was encouraged to explore the magic of computing and discover just how contemporary the Sai phenomenon is.

The initial investigation of the writings on Sai Baba proved tiresome, until some anecdotes shared by the same lady worker brought them to life. What began as a chore developed into genuine fascination and I slowly came to grasp that I wasn't really writing a book on the Sai saints at all. Instead, something in me was being prompted to write about a reality that their lives reflected and I was being subtly made to understand that this study was a means of grace by which my own soul could reach nearer to the Sai realization. Despite the fact that Shirdi and Sathya Sai Baba belong to apparently different faiths and very different times, the fact that they both were born in the Deccan—Shirdi in the Marathi-speaking north and Puttaparthi in the Telugu-speaking south—can be seen as symbolic, both of the oneness underlying their being and the process of unification they embodied in their lives. Like Guru Nanak, they are revered for being consciously eclectic, preferring a more human, tender and lyrical approach to religion, one that is kinder on the self. Their approach to the spirit has always emphasized genuine inner understanding over asceticism.

This realization of mine was followed by small but meaningful incidents which forced me to accept that psychic visiting cards were being left by the Sai Parampara (Sai tradition) to ease my journey. Once, within minutes of paying out Rs 2,800 in cash for a back-up computer battery, I received a letter containing a cheque for Rs 2,850. For a Scotsman in a mofussil town like Mussoorie, where courier services are a hit-and-miss affair (at least a dozen properties on our hillside include 'oak' in their name), this is the best evidence of things unseen at work! A telephone call from a friend would mention a book and, remembering I had another one by the same author, I would go to a forgotten bookshelf and find a title there that would contribute to my research. While writing this book, I tried in vain to recall the name of the author whose extraordinarily vivid account of his time with Sai Baba I had once read. On submitting the manuscript, out of the blue my publisher David Davidar asked me if I had read *Empire of the Soul* by his friend Paul William Roberts—the very name which had escaped me. A week later, while browsing in the local bookshop, what do I spot in the discount section but *Empire of the Soul*, standing alongside K.A. Nilakanta Sastri's *A History of South India*, a seminal account of the 'aryanization' of the Deccan. These could be called coincidences, but to encounter two a day sometimes, and that too over a period of several months, suggested the hand of grace. One day, of their own accord, three boldly underlined sentences in large type appeared on the computer screen, summarizing precisely what my writing was trying to say:

> There is only one last word and that is love. Love not as a doctrinal extra but a necessary tool that alone can effect any transformation. Not even the finest philosophy can work without love. Only love delivers us beyond all life's questions. This is the one grace worth having and that is why rich and poor alike, overcoming the difficulties of the way repair to Puttaparthi.

This study of grace, as reflected in the form of Sathya Sai Baba, is but one of dozens that have been penned and makes no claims whatever to any special insights. In 1945, the young Sathya Sai composed a poem in which he talked about 'self-puffed pseudo-dons'; I have an uncomfortable suspicion that he was referring to writers like me. My approach may differ slightly in that I seek to place the emphasis for any transformation by grace on the efforts of the devotee rather than on his resigned wait for divine beneficence to fall about his ears. We sally forth to do battle on the understanding that the outcome is not in our hands. However, our individual input can affect the outcome, which is why it is important for the devotee to try and meet the guru halfway.

This study views the Sai Parampara from the standpoint of a sympathetic outsider—one who wants to convey the remarkable power of love at work but who, at the same time, is willing to answer the criticisms that any such large-scale movement attracts. Central to my thesis is the observation that the Sai Parampara represents a more democratic rendering of divinity than has been customary.

I will argue that these two saints of the Deccan have not only softened our concept of God, but have also strengthened the claim of humanism to share space with the sacrosanct. The divine, in this instance, emerged from the ordinary (Sathya Sai's birth in the farmer Pedda Venkappa Raju's household) and, significantly, the spirit travelled from the lower to the higher—in opposition to the conventional direction preferred by religion. Only when the commonplace has been visibly made divine—as appears to have happened in Shirdi and Puttaparthi—can its claim to embodying the oneness of all realms be taken seriously and its declared mission of compassion examined for its source of energy.

The development of religious understanding since the days of ancient Egypt has seen a spatial descent from the head to the heart, relocating divine power from the Pharaoh to a carpenter who rode a donkey. The tender graces of religion have made mankind recognize that love in the heart is a surer sign of divinity than any worldly display of power. The Sai Parampara emphasizes the presence of the spirit in ordinary life and enthrones human love in the sacred space formerly reserved for a divine potentate. Probably for the first time in the history of theology, the devotee is no longer bound by the convention of using the upper case when talking of the divine. Sai Parampara has removed the priestly middleman from the devotee's equation with the divine.

The bulk of the modern Sai following (both in India and elsewhere) is nearer to middle than lower class. What makes the Sai Parampara attractive is its promise of direct contact with the spirit, irrespective of the follower's economic status, and its readiness to experiment with an

unorthodox approach to divinity. All sorts of people
mingle at Shirdi and Puttaparthi and they have made the
long journey not for religious reasons but to satisfy their
soul with the live experience of love.

This humanizing of the sacred being is suggested
more forcefully by Sathya Sai Baba's physical relocation
of the seat of divinity from what the poet Larkin calls
'the holy end'. What surprises the visitor to Puttaparthi
the most is not the absence of priests but the omission of
a sanctum sanctorum where offerings are made. The
absence of a house of worship breaks new theological
ground, going against the hallowed tradition that the
divine needs its own space, whether in heaven or on
consecrated earth. The Protestant faith in Europe
challenged the validity of priestly middlemen, but the Sai
Parampara goes one step further and removes the holy
ground from under their feet. (Certain Protestant sects do
dispense with formal 'fixing' of the divine to a specific
location. However they usually consider their meeting
places as 'set apart'.) Both Shirdi and Sathya Sai point to
the human heart as the only true temple since this is
where love resides.

'My definition of love,' says Sathya Sai, 'is to redress
the sufferings of the poor and needy.' Sai Baba gives
directly to the deprived, cutting out the administrative
expenses that swallow so much official funding. This
'science of the spirit' indicates the concern of a modern
reformer who has had to wait patiently for sixty years
before his mission could win over and then outgrow
religious orthodoxy.

The liberating universality of the Sai vision can be
experienced first-hand when you stand overlooking the

pink and green Puttaparthi hills from Chaitanya Jyoti, a modern structure built in 2000 to celebrate Sathya Sai Baba's seventy-fifth birthday. This exciting architectural edifice combines the features of a traditional Chinese temple with contemporary Islamic domes. Prior to this, Sai Baba's ashram was seen by many as just another centre for the mobilization of the Hindu masses. However, what has really been mobilized by Sai Baba is the spirit, reclaimed like Promethean fire from the confines of orthodoxy.

To this observer, the Sai Parampara expresses the truly Indian instinct of welcoming plurality (as opposed to the orthodox Hindu attitude of tolerating it). Its universal message is not based on textual clichés regarding the oneness of things. Instead, it derives from the experiencing of multiple identities as witnessed in the contrasting figures of Shirdi and Sathya Sai. Traditional Eastern wisdom asserts that the soul is reborn in order to experience the entire range of human possibilities. The best example of this is the remarkable life of Ramakrishna Paramhansa who actually lived out the disciplines of different faiths, adopting sincerely the dress, customs and observances of the followers of Christianity, Islam and other religions. Likewise, in Puttaparthi the celebration of Christmas, for example, is not a patronizing imitation of an alien tradition but an utterly genuine celebration of the birth of the spirit.

To try and bring home the universal spiritual lineage of these modern saints, I have invoked comparisons with modern masters, especially by drawing on the life and teachings of the strange and sometimes outlandish George Gurdjieff, who at first may seem to be the antithesis of

Sathya Sai and the Sai Parampara. The fact is that the Sufi teaching methods of Shirdi Baba were distinctly outlandish and, like Gurdjieff, he believed in shock therapy. Both could demand *dakshina* (payment) from their disciples. Gurdjieff's immoderate demands were a deliberate ploy to sort the genuine seeker from the merely fashionable follower. To the world at large, Gurdjieff appears a cynic. But his select following, which included some of the western world's outstanding litterateurs, produced a handful of remarkable books that convey his true spiritual stature, notwithstanding anything his behaviour may have suggested. Like Shirdi Baba, he was a Sufi free of the conventions that came in the way of the recognition of the oneness of the spirit. Gurdjieff hailed from Armenia and, although born a Christian, he travelled widely in search of Eastern wisdom. He founded the Institute for the Harmonious Development of Man near Paris and died in 1947, leaving behind a small following that has increased, like Shirdi Baba's, on the strength of the teacher's continuing presence. Like all true teachers—and there have been surprisingly few in the history of religion—he spoke with an authority that was not his own. Yet, paradoxically, the source of that authority seemed to come from his inner self. (Sathya Sai, despite appearances, can also behave unpredictably and display an authority that seems whimsical until its long-term benefits are appreciated.)

*

Unlike many of my friends, I like the world the way the Almighty has made it. I have no regrets about the wayward course my life has taken since that has enabled me to take an original angle on things. Born in central Scotland, sent to school in the English Midlands, then on to university in Yorkshire, I have lived in Calcutta, the Kumaun hills, Delhi and Garhwal, thus acquiring the identity of a near nomad. One good thing about a Scottish upbringing is the ingrained response to the overpowering beauty of nature which allows a lot of pre-Christian paganism to shine through. I rather like the term 'heathen' and as a boy, loved to tramp over the moors, marvelling at the miracle of the heather. My soul responded rapturously to the Ochil foothills and I was brought up to believe in fairies and ghosts. To the first I offered any broken tooth along with a three-penny piece and a pinch of salt thrown over the shoulder. Ghosts were a sad reminder of Highland laddies fallen in war and no one, it seemed to me, with a sense of pity and the gift of the second sight, could doubt the reality of the psychic realm.

It was traumatic to leave the hills of my birthplace to attend grammar school in the industrial city of Birmingham. But while there, my religion was identified for me by a famous preacher who came to deliver a sermon at St. Martin's in the Bull Ring. It was a fine Sunday morning, but the church was as dank and musty as a jail. The clergyman thundered against those who betrayed their Christian heritage and journeyed out of the city instead of attending church. He called them 'Blue Domers' because they preferred to celebrate God's presence under the blue dome of heaven. Thanks to this preacher I would later discover that there was no need for me to attend church again. He had reintroduced me to my heathen heritage.

I once toyed with the idea of joining the church and becoming an ordained minister. As an exercise, I travelled all over Britain, assessing various orders, seeking a religion that would answer my soul's needs. I stayed at a Franciscan friary in Dorset but was much more impressed by the huge phallic figure carved into the hillside by pagan Britons. I dined at High Anglican community tables but came away appalled at the prospect of a lifetime spent discussing theology with the smell of pickled onions on one's breath. Religion proved itself to be a big bore and seeing all the half-empty churches, I concluded that the Almighty had joined the ranks of the Sunday truants and fled to enjoy the blue dome of heaven.

My quest was to find the meaning of true religion and to this end I studied comparative religion at Leeds University. According to my guru at Mirtola, people who study comparative religion are only comparatively religious and this was proved by the fact that almost all the views expressed on the oriental religions were from a missionary perspective. Yet, this was better than nothing. In Britain, almost all chairs of theology were confined to Christian incumbents and Leeds was unique in having been founded, in large part, with Jewish money earned from the wool trade. Not unnaturally, the donors endowed a professorship not hostile to any particular faith. In spite of their bias, my lecturers were not able to entirely downplay the beauties of Hinduism which my eclectic soul detected to be crucial for the completeness of its education.

The faith that came nearest to what I was looking for was practised by the Theosophical Society with its conviction about the essential unity of all religions.

However, when I visited Adyar, the headquarters of the movement, in 1960, there didn't seem to be much going on. It took fifteen more years of searching before I found what I was looking for—in the newly built Sarva Dharma Stupa of Sathya Sai Baba at Prasanthi Nilayam, an eclectic column that reaffirmed the oneness of life's informing spirit through various facets of the world's living religions. Here was the oneing process made public, the '*Sab ka malik ek* (There is but one divine master)' creed of the Sai Parampara openly declared. It felt like a homecoming after years of being at sea.

Within a month of completing my master's degree (on Mahatma Gandhi's karma yoga), I set off hitchhiking round the world to experience at first-hand those religions of the East whose doctrines I had studied. The overland journey lasted two months and enabled me to see holy sites like Istanbul, Jerusalem, Nazareth, Isfahan, Amritsar and Benares (now Varanasi), opening a small window on how the world's great living religions conducted their affairs. What is both embarrassing and annoying in retrospect is that I travelled through Anatolia (in Turkey) and Tabriz (in Iran) entirely unaware of the spiritual greatness of the Sufi teacher Jalalluddin Rumi. I now realize that instead of visiting the conventional pilgrimage sites of the Holy Land, I should have looked in the 'district of joy' (as Andrew Harvey puts it) where the world's greatest mystic had taught the path of love, which he called the art of getting drunk without wine.

Rumi understood the real value of things and would have approved of Sai Baba's avowal: 'If you can earn my grace it is as good as getting the entire world.' Grace can strike us from any direction, though it would be wrong to assume that it is as random as lightning. One has to be at the right place at the right time for the flame to ignite and these junctures are rarely arrived at by fatalistic acquiescence. Usually, decisions have led us there and, more often than not, the decisions have been hard, involving much wrestling with the soul even though the situation may have seemed trivial at the time. The grace of love is less likely to zap the armchair traveller than the adventurer. While hitchhiking to India, on several occasions, only an unshakable faith in the hand of Providence saw me through the long waits when traffic was thin and the soul was forced to accept that one is entirely dependent on the grace of the creator. But challenging this traditional view are the words of Sathya Sai: 'All this grace would be of no avail if you do not secure the grace of your inner consciousness.'

My journey to India was marked by a minor grace that began and finished the adventure. While writing my thesis I had taken a teaching job in Birmingham and when my class heard of my plans to travel to India, they presented me with a copy of Paul Brunton's *A Search in Secret India*, a book that introduced Sri Ramana Maharishi to the western reader. Uncannily, on arrival in Calcutta, I found a teaching job in the very school where Arthur Osborne, the biographer of Ramana Maharishi, used to be the principal. It seemed some blessing was at work to guide my search. After a year of teaching at Hindi High School, I moved to the Himalayas. Sarala Devi, an English disciple of Gandhiji, said I could be the odd-job man at her crafts school for girls in Kausani. The opportunity to live in sight of the great snow peaks proved irresistible after a year spent in Calcutta's urban clutter. Sarala was a person of rare integrity. Apart from Sathya Sai Baba, she is the only person I have ever met who practises exactly what she preaches. It was thanks to Sarala's advice that I found my guru and, luckily for my soul (which found great comfort in the inspiration of the Himalayas), his ashram was not far from Kausani.

The seven years I spent in Mirtola are more memorable for the shedding of unreal parts than for the acquiring of grace. The ashram was centred around the divine love of Radha–Krishna as the symbol of the only real thing. My gurus, Sri Krishna Prem and Sri Madhav Ashish, referred to themselves as pupil–teachers and their teaching aimed to demonstrate through hard physical and emotional exercises that we are more than the body. The real man, they insisted, is at all times aware of the immortal spirit burning within. I have, over the years, come to see this description fulfilled in Sathya Sai Baba. In the beginning, however, my eyes were firmly closed to this reality and only grace can explain how they were slowly opened.

2

Love as the Guide

Nobody seems to know the correct etymology of the word 'religion', and maybe this is as it should be, because religion deals with the numinous relationship between humans and the life force that brought them forth into a wondrous and mysterious universe. Ideally, religion should teach us responsibility for our behaviour and the Protestant movement in Europe, redefining the relevance of the priestly intermediary between the individual soul and God, was a step in that direction. A thousand years before Luther, however, the Bhakti movement, with its roots in south India, rose to challenge the necessity of ritual. The roots of the Sai Parampara lie in this bypassing of ritual Brahminism. When it spread north, this movement sought to reconcile the new egalitarian force of Islam with unorthodox Hindu beliefs.

True religion is hard to put into words. The best definition I have found is Sathya Sai's: 'Divinity exploring its own wonders.' This implies that real religion lies within and is activated by our human concern for others. In the words of St. James, the brother of Christ, 'Pure and undefiled religion is to visit the fatherless and widows in their affliction and to keep himself unspotted from the world.' He is emphasizing the importance of demonstrating compassion to the needy. We seldom take this simple formula of helping those in need beyond our family circle, though it should be noted that in some numerically smaller faiths there is a conscious effort to extend this succour at least to fellow members of the community. Thus, Parsis, Sikhs or Jains are rarely known to beg because of their strong sense of identity and the efficacy of their charitable arrangements.

As an example of true religion I can quote the story of a Sikh taxi driver travelling on the Mumbai–Pune highway. A Parsi guru-behn (sister disciple) of mine was on a holiday with her husband and children, driving a small car with a heavily loaded roof-rack, a factor she forgot to take into account when she pulled out to overtake. The sluggish car met with a head-on collision. My friend and her family members were thrown out violently and ended up, most of them dead, in a field. The passing Sikh stopped his taxi, rescued the survivors— the mother and her baby—and drove them to hospital. Sadly, the baby died but the Sikh would come to visit the unconscious mother daily. He kept coming till she regained consciousness, then ceased to visit, and she never found out who her deliverer was. (Often, in miraculous interventions recounted by Sai devotees, they find that their deliverer was Sai Baba in the guise of a common man.)

The extraordinary thing about mankind is that despite the expanding horizons of knowledge and information, we understand very little about our individual identity or about the divine consciousness which the mystics of all religions affirm we are a part of. However, thanks to the openness of the Hindu mind and its genuine desire to solve the riddle of existence, India has long been the laboratory for experiments in religious unity. No other country can match the Indian record of tolerance of a wide range of approaches to the divine. Thus, along with the strife caused by those who exploit religion for personal or political motives, there has always been an undercurrent of harmony between individuals of different faiths in the subcontinent.

In the recent past, one of the best examples of this real but unheralded unity has been the sweeping popularity of the figure of Sai Baba—both in the guise of Shirdi Sai Baba, depicted as an old fakir in torn clothes, and the Puttaparthi Sathya Sai, a (no longer) young saint characteristically represented in a long orange robe sporting an Afro-style halo of hair. Millions worldwide worship both saints as part of a continuing Sai Parampara according to which there will be three saints in all. Prem Sai, the third avatar, is predicted to come after Sathya Sai. Though his father is believed to be born already, the son is not expected to declare himself until the passing of Sri Sathya Sai who predicts that his earthly span will be ninety-six years. Each of these masters, though assumed by many to be one on a psychic plane, is associated with a separate ashram each at Shirdi, Puttaparthi, and, in the future, at Gunaparthi (Mysore) respectively.

The symbolism of the Sai trinity dates from 1940 (the year Sathyanarayan Raju announced he was Sai Baba) when a coconut offered in a local temple broke into three pieces. Puttaparthi lore signifies this as a prediction of three avataric figures in the Sai Parampara, echoing the trinity motif enshrined in the ashram mythology which explains how rishi Bharadwaj had journeyed to Kailash to seek the blessings of Shiva and Parvati. The latter, busily engaged in a dancing marathon, kept the rishi waiting and as reparation for their preoccupation they offered him three boons, descending to bless earth in three separate incarnations of the divine. The first would be Shiva as Shirdi Sai, the second Shiva and Parvati together as Sathya Sai and the third, still to appear, Parvati as Prem Sai.

Dr S.P. Ruhela's book, *The Sai Trinity* (1994), gathers together what little, and obviously hypothetical, information is available on the subject. (The book is valuable if only for its exhaustive bibliography.) Though only six pages of information are forthcoming on the third incarnation of Sai, they provide a mine of interesting leads. Devotees claim to have heard mention of the third Sai since 1950 and a public acknowledgement was made by Sathya Sai in 1963. It was predicted that he will be born on the banks of the Kaveri in Mandya district (Karnataka) in the first quarter of the new century. John Hislop, Baba's American disciple, was gifted a ring with the image of Prem Sai which roughly approximates to the imagined face of Christ. In his interviews with chosen disciples, Sathya Sai has elaborated on aspects of his forthcoming successor. As this information is intended for specific devotees' ears and may have symbolic meanings only the hearer can understand, we should resist the urge to take these private confidences literally.

The aim of this study is to emphasize the underlying

unity of the Sai figures and demonstrate that the grace that flows from them derives from the same compassionate source. So I have used the term 'Sai Parampara' (line of saints, apostolic succession) throughout to refer loosely to their common spiritual purpose and not to any formal order of mendicants (sampradaya). However, I know that this bracketing of convenience will not find favour with certain Shirdi devotees who refuse to acknowledge any connection with Sathya Sai. Though, as the latter's mission increases in its good works, many formerly hostile are now sympathetic to the idea of a continuity in teaching, if not in persona. The fact remains that a separation of identities does not affect the theological commonality between Shirdi Sai and Sathya Sai. Going by the sum of the (admittedly amorphous) evidence, I find no compelling reason not to regard Sathya Sai Baba as a spiritual encore of the Shirdi fakir. For most, this is a matter of belief. For a student who wants to examine how grace works, physical differences are irrelevant. Whatever garment grace may choose to wear, it is crucial to focus on the inner content and view the outer form as a vehicle of reality, not reality itself.

To offset criticism by the newer devotees of Shirdi Sai, there is a considerable amount of testimony from old Shirdi bhaktas which confirms that the fakir's spiritual continuity is invested in Sathya Sai. Once, while passing through Mangalore, I visited the shop of Shri Krishna Shet, a jeweller who, as a boy, had been taken by his father to have darshan of Shirdi Baba. The boy was given the job of feeding Shirdi's pet dog Manohar, who appears prominently in the early portraits of the saint. Many years later, when Krishna Shet decided to visit Puttaparthi, the first question Sathya Sai asked him was, 'Where is Manohar?'

What is remarkable about the Sai saints is that despite their indifference to cult following or floating a new religious movement, their grace continues to spread of its own volition, without any funding or missionary endeavour. Ordinary people of any religion, caste or community are free to consider themselves Sai devotees, without any need of a formal initiation. The only requirement is a burning love for, and faith in, Sai Baba as your personal guru. In return, you are not expected to be a Sai Baba-ist but a good Hindu, Christian or Muslim or whatever your parent religion happens to be. Does this loyalty to the Sai movement mean conflict with the parent religion? The answer is that every religion has a mystical core to which serious enquirers gravitate. Because the number of Sai devotees is still limited, relatively speaking, there is little cause to provoke any official backlash from any organized religion. Though, it must be said here that when Don Mario Mazzoleni, a Catholic priest who worked for Vatican Radio, published *A Catholic Priest Meets Sai Baba* (1994) in which he revealed that he had found the essence of Christ in the Puttaparthi master, he was swiftly and unceremoniously excommunicated.

The Sai movement, with its uncomplicated theology and insistence on experiencing love, is based on a fresh interpretation of the Upanishadic insights of classical Hinduism, which, after a millennium, were endorsed by the Sufi exponents of Islam as well as by mystics of other faiths. The revolutionary achievement of the Sai Parampara is to have demonstrated the truth of the immanent nature

of the divine and make it accessible to the ordinary
seeker. What it audaciously claims is the experience of all
mystics:

> Hear O man, sole root of sin in thee
> Is not to know thine own divinity.

The message is as profound as it is simple but the path
for the seeker is perilous, with a high rate of casualty.

*

In ancient Greece, the words 'Know Thyself' were written
above the gates of the Academy, the school of knowledge
and wisdom in Athens. This insight also contains the
essence of classical Hindu religious thought as enunciated
in the Upanishads. Applicable to the individual spirit, the
search for the divine within was overlaid by the Hebraic
concern for collective moral responsibility. And so we
have Judaism's emphasis on the transcendental aspect of
the divine. This viewing of life in stark black and white
was adopted by both its monotheistic offspring,
Christianity and Islam. The civilizational advance of
Christendom and Islam reduced the ancient Indian teaching
to a species of pagan heresy. Though the inquiry into the
self continued in Europe under the guise of the alchemical
search for gold, the monotheistic establishment thought
nothing of snuffing out any individual soul who challenged
its notion of a distant divinity. The Judaic concept that
the divine was separate from nature diminished the latter
and introduced the reckless assumption that man was the
indisputable master of his physical environment. The
ecological degradation of our wondrous planet is in part

the fallout of this misunderstanding of the divine status of nature.

By overstressing the superiority of the creator over his creation, Judaism's doctrine denied to the soul the beauty and inspiration of the natural world. And the idea of 'original sin' degraded the human body and the sexual act responsible for reproduction to a permanent state of spiritual deprivation. (Significantly, the canonical credentials of the Song of Solomon, where the physical power of love is broached, have been the object of puritanical suspicion down the ages.)

Every person who has been in love experiences a oneness with the beloved that can only be described as divine, and to achieve that moment of realization is to tread holy ground. In the opposite state of evil, we are separated from the oneness. As George Orwell demonstrates in *Nineteen Eighty-Four*, when love is betrayed, we distance ourselves from the divine within us.

Love's promptings arouse awe rather than guilt and this is why the Sai Parampara appeals to all who value the teaching: 'Perfect love casteth out fear'. Love, because it fuels the wonder of being, is a greater mystery than God. If this seems too heretical for conventional religion to stomach, the truth can be reformulated to suggest that God (to all but atheists) is love objectified. Sathya Sai Baba does not insist that his followers must be 'believers' nor indeed that they be 'followers'. In fact, he often declares that his portrayal of the divine as universal love is of benefit to believer and non-believer alike. To insist, as the Sai Parampara does, that love is beyond the reach of formal religion is a revolutionary spiritual insight.

Perhaps the most graceful exponent of the Upanishadic

approach was Sri Ramana Maharishi who radiated the benevolence of divine immanence from his seat in south India under the sacred Arunachala mountain. One must add here that the Vedantic school of Hindu orthodoxy shares the misgivings of the Jews about the wondrous place of nature. Its doctrine of maya which denies reality to the material world is another example of the distorting theology which has been vigorously countered in India by the Bhakti schools' celebration of the wonder of the everyday world.

Not very far from Ramana's ashram, the Puttaparthi campus that came up after his death in 1951 went on to echo his teaching. This is quite remarkable given that Ramana taught an uncompromising Advaitic notion of divinity by the rigorous method of continual self-questioning. By contrast, the saint of Puttaparthi would stress the bhakti approach of singing God's name and performing acts of charity as the best means to fix the mind in godliness. How could these outwardly conflicting paths possibly converge? The truth is that the inclusive instinct of Hinduism allows easy room for such theological manoeuvring. Ramana, no doubt, was seen as a stern exponent of Advaita Vedanta, but at the same time he was an ardent bhakta who wrote lyrical hymns to his beloved Arunachala, the pillar of light which had drawn him to its feet. In the very first installment of his *Prem Vahini* (1958), Sathya Sai wrote categorically: 'There is no distinction between bhakti and jnana.'

Despite his initial reservations about the status of Sathya Sai, Arthur Osborne took to him warmly as a worthy successor to his guru Ramana Maharishi. This was not surprising. When I first stayed with the Osbornes, it was clear from the outset that they adored their guru with pure bhakti and this feeling swamped every other, including the doctrinal niceties of Advaita. The whole mood of Ramanashram was of vibrant bhakti that affirmed the insights of Vedanta. Likewise, visitors to Shirdi have been astonished to find the intermingling of both bhakti and Advaita. The same can be said for Puttaparthi, though, because of the mass gathering, the Advaita component may not be as obvious here.

When I first visited Puttaparthi in the late 1970s, I was overtaken by a sense of familiarity, the place was so reminiscent of Ramanashram. The silence here was not the negative discipline of keeping mum but rather the realized mood that comes with energies consciously directed. At last I had found the religion that Rumi professed, straight from the heart and free of the elaborate theological doctrine of conventional religion. The Sai Parampara appeals directly to the spiritual centre, our seat of awareness which feels compassionate oneness with all of life. There is no need to convert mankind; the very word 'kind' suggests it is our deepest nature to bond with others. Neither Shirdi nor Sathya Sai Baba concern themselves unduly with doctrine: it is by stimulating awareness that the seeker's veil of ignorance is removed. It is to this untapped spiritual part, beyond the reach of divisive labels, that Sai Baba appeals.

*

The Sai phenomenon is viewed as an avatar, an incarnation of God by many disciples, but to some, Sai is the Godhead itself. Imponderables such as the nature of the divine or the attributes of an avatar are beyond the ken of the average enquirer. However, to anyone blessed with the maddening experience of love, at least a ray of light is available for viewing such imponderables. When love smiles, our understanding is strangely enhanced. Love gives wings to the seeker. The Sathya Sai phenomenon makes sense only to a lover or to those who, like Kipling's Kim, 'wonder what manner of thing their soul might be'. Through love we can experience the mystery of the divine, a realization that is on an entirely different plane from the fruits of any intellectual analysis. In one of its few spiritual insights, the English language likens the impact of love to a 'fall', implying a perilous descent into an abyss of untold splendour.

Understanding divinity can be made easier by reconciling some of the claims of scripture with the findings of science. In *The Origin of Species*, which upset the applecart of biblical chronology, Darwin's discoveries about human evolution suggest that the divine author of the universe is still struggling to know 'itself'. From the imperfection of nature and the violence of its warring parts, we can only grasp at the flower of compassion and think of it as the ultimate destination towards which all of life's energies are stumbling.

The experience of human love, with its terrible accompaniment of suffering, can be confirmed as a divine energy by Darwin's halting theory. The perfection of the Godhead cannot be lived out fully on earth even by an avatar. But flickerings from that all-powerful source offer glimpses to the seeker who loves, just as they illumine most of the avatar's actions. Love stands beyond all theories and operates according to its own laws, one of which seems to be that human imperfection, paradoxically, is made perfect by its power. The fact that human love seems imperfect does not make it any less miraculous. The twin saints of the Deccan, Shirdi and Sathya Sai, attribute all the miracles they are famous for to the divine nature of love.

Love may be the goal of religion, but you can spend a lifetime wading through scriptures and theological commentaries trying to establish this simple truth. Too often, it comes with the small print suggesting that the divine power likes (or does not like) to be loved with (or more often without) hats, shoes, unstitched garments, onions, meat, drink, tobacco, shaven heads, beards, etc. The baffling irrationality of religious codes is in contrast to the unswerving spiritual awareness practised by true saints who remain indifferent to these restrictions. This is clearly demonstrated in the lives of the Deccan saints. Shirdi Baba stayed for sixty years in the same setting, ensconced in his Dwarkamayi mosque (a Muslim sanctuary with a Hindu name), unperturbed by spiritual vetoes. Similarly, Sathya Sai gives darshan outside his Prasanthi Nilayam 'mandir' (which is actually a prayer hall) just as he has done continuously for the past seventy years, unruffled by the concerns of religious propriety.

The Sai Parampara gives darshan the highest priority and in both Shirdi and Puttaparthi all activities are centred round this public mystery. Many who ask for a summary of the Sai teachings are flummoxed by being referred to this living doctrine of darshan. It is both the central communion and the theology of the movement. It explains why there is no sanctum sanctorum either at Shirdi or Puttaparthi and why there is no holy book or creed. Some confuse darshan with a personality cult but blind belief is antithetical to the Sai Parampara. Sathya Sai never sits on any designated throne save to bless it. When arati is offered, he takes good care not to receive it personally except for the initial acknowledgement of the love that occasions it. Sai Baba's darshan embodies love. As the celebrated yogi Suddhananda Bharati (who spent time with both Shirdi and Sathya Sai) noted at Venkatagiri in 1958, 'Living with Sai Baba is samadhi.'

The glow one feels during a Sai darshan is the experiencing of this paradox which the mind finds hard to accept but the heart knows to be true. Away from Sai's presence, our imperfection is almost too painful to behold, hence the provision of photographs, medallions and other seemingly trivial mementos of Sai Baba that help bridge the gap caused by his (the spirit's) absence. Hence, too, the discipline of sitting long hours in Puttaparthi, building up the longing of the heart for its moment of re-contact with the divine. Our souls are too unpractised to carry the divine charge for more than a few hours, though constant application can prolong the lingering of love's fragrance.

According to Sathya Sai, 'God sleeps in the mineral, wakes in the vegetable, walks in the animal and thinks in man.' True religion, he argues, is the 'religion of man'. We are born to seek enlightenment (which will disperse the superstitions practised by conventionally religious people) and recognize the oneness of life, the same immortal spirit in the high and the low. The most compelling definition of enlightenment lies not in theological exposition but in experiencing the grace of falling in love. The difference between the religious and the spiritual person is in the experiencing of love. Love is the poor man's self-realization. It is an all-enveloping fire that consumes the divisiveness of religious ideologies. Having studied religion for a lifetime, I find more love in songs written by pop stars than in sermons delivered from lofty pulpits. Religion is feudal, love democratic. Religion binds with briars while love is the freedom to be ourselves. Religion reduces life to a boring duty while love is an exploding wonder that makes the most ordinary activity seem miraculous. Religion represents the dead weight of the past while love is an ever-present grace. The demand of the Sai Parampara that we obey the dictates of love and surrender our assumptions, dogma and intellectual pride is realistic because the only thing most of us do readily surrender to is the power of love.

Some may argue this is a rich man's sport and that love is beyond the pinched circumstances of the poor. Self-recollection and the singing of bhajans hardly contribute to the world's welfare, it is argued, and most of us employed during the day have no time to sit idle and contemplate divinity. More often than not these are excuses made by the monkey mind to avoid the hard work involved in knowing the self and fighting the senses. Only when the follies of the mind have been exposed do we begin to understand that it behaves like a clever lawyer, infinitely acrobatic in its skill. It seeks to fool its owner that it is a more reliable organ than the heart when it comes to understanding reality.

Along with the devotees there is another category of seeker which flocks to Sai Baba, the kind suffering from insolvable problems or terminal diseases. Even 'rationalists' will bring along a loved one who is dying

and beyond the skills of conventional cure in the hope
that Sai Baba will work a miracle, though that will in
effect demolish their philosophy. Sadly, many people who
could be helped by the reservoir of love generated at a
Puttaparthi darshan decline the opportunity due to
intellectual reservations. These arise from an attendant
irritant to the Sai phenomena—the devotional excesses of
some followers who make ridiculous claims and see
miracles where none exist. For instance, the neurotic
transmitting of chain letters by some devotees which urge
the receiver to keep up the communication link for fear
of something untoward happening has annoyed the public
and cheapened the name of the movement. The story of
the Sai Parampara thus has to be prised out of the
extreme views of opposite camps—those who worship
blindly and swallow the most absurd assumptions, and
those doubters and cynics who assume only delusion,
profiteering and superstition to be at work.

*

My first acquaintance with the Sai phenomenon was
thanks to the benign guidance of Arthur Osborne, a
devotee who had achieved the rare union of sharp intellect
with devotional warmth. Then, later in the nineteen-
sixties, during my stint in the Himalayan ashram of
Mirtola, in the days when I believed a hair)shirt would
hasten my quest for enlightenment, a beautiful exotic
woman, Prithwi, Maharani of Jind, arrived. I first saw
her just as I was swatting hornets that had attacked our
beehives. I fell so madly in love with this vision of
feminine loveliness that I got badly stung by the hornets!

My guru, a man of extraordinary understanding, there and then handed over the charge of my inner education to the new arrival. 'Love is the guide,' he argued, and the only certain way to find real religion is to hitch your wagon to that star.

Rani-ma's name means 'Mother Earth' and she possesses the unique gift of feeling perfectly at home in any situation, worldly or otherwise. Her intensity of devotion allows her to steamroll her way into the hearts of all but those who are jealous of her gift of outspokenness. Like many Punjabis, her natural exuberance is often mistaken by the more culturally sensitive as bordering on the audacious, but this ability to get inside the armour of others is her greatest strength. It enables her to love holy men, for example, both for their holiness and their manliness, something which is unique.

The Mirtola ashram, where I had been living, was not on the 'Godman' circuit of the swinging sixties and most of the information about contemporary saints and frauds came from the reports of visitors. To many visitors, Mirtola suffered from the reputation of being too intellectual in its approach and, while this was not true of the gurus there, it certainly applied to many of the disciples, including myself. To balance things, the routine at this self-sufficient ashram was so physically exhausting that it would have been deemed masochistic save for the conscious inspiration of the Gurdjieffian axiom: 'Better to die than live in sleep.' Or, as the mountaineer–author Rene Daumal put it, 'It is vitally important to find out before we die why we were born.'

Presumably, Sri Sathya Sai found Rani-ma's approach to his widely acclaimed divine status a welcome change.

Most of his devotees regard him with awe verging on trepidation, but she responds to his human warmth and is not afraid to disagree with him on occasion. In his ashram she is simply known as Rani-ma. Rani-ma's down-to-earth attitude enabled her to spot genuine religion long before it would pass the intellectual filters of Mirtola. Our guru Ashishda, for example, was chary of accepting her assessment of the Bombay saint Nisarga Datta (who in the 1960s was affectionately referred to as 'Bidi Maharaj' from his habit of smoking and selling bidis). Later, Ashishda drastically revised his opinion of Nisarga Datta and would extol him as one of the greatest practitioners of the art of enlightenment. When Rani-ma introduced us to her master, Sai Baba, we were very sceptical of his genuineness. Newspaper articles about him harped on his display of psychic powers and in his speeches he openly declared himself to be God. His odd appearance and Afro hairstyle also worked against him and the most we at Mirtola would grant him was the status of a charismatic cheerleader of the masses, possessing the appeal of a Mahatma Gandhi. I moved out of Mirtola in 1972 and had my first darshan of Sai Baba at Rani-ma's house in Delhi that winter. Without question, his was the most electrifying presence of any holy man or, for that matter, any human being I had ever met (or have met since). He seemed to crackle with psychic static as though charged with an energy so vital that you would receive a shock if you touched him. Now I understood why Rani-ma claimed that she visited his then primitive ashram in the backwoods of Puttaparthi to recharge her batteries.

It was her son Bharat who had first come into contact

with Sathya Sai in the early 1960s. Bharat was one of the last of the charming breed of princes, a golden-hearted teenaged pensioner who drank away his fortune. Yet, in a short span of life, he left more fragrant memories than most people of a religious disposition achieve if they live to be a hundred. Perhaps recognizing Bharat's purity of heart, Sai Baba had offered to put him in charge of the development of Puttaparthi, which in the 1960s comprised only of incipient ashram buildings adjacent to the impoverished village.

Rani-ma describes how Baba had told her of his big plans to put Puttaparthi on the world map. He had just got back from Uganda, his one and, to date, only overseas visit. She recalls how she also didn't pay heed when Baba described his vision of a university, an airport, a hospital and a thriving township in the sparse Rayalseema outback they surveyed together on a drive to Anantapur in 1968. He had asked Rani-ma and Bharat to wait by the roadside outside Puttaparthi (to avoid attracting attention) and then drove up to collect them in a battered old car with one other passenger, a sitting judge. Baba was going to buy land at Anantapur to build a college for girls, beginning an extraordinary development programme in the fields of education, medicine and culture. Rani-ma remembers how the money was 'produced' before the tehsildar and how Baba insisted that her son should join the work of turning the wilderness into a land of milk and honey. But Bharat felt that it was beyond his wayward lifestyle.

Despite the charged aura that I had experienced on my first meeting with Baba, like most other ordinary seekers, I felt excluded from the magic circle of Sai devotees. The price of having Sai Baba as a guru was to surrender entirely to him in love. For an intellectual this seemed a risky investment at best, a Faustian gamble with one's soul. And to harden my feelings was the blind adoration of many of the devotees who believed that everything Baba said and did was of miraculous import. During that first darshan in Delhi, I attended a public discourse by Baba delivered before an audience of the capital's VIPs. Baba spoke vivaciously enough in Telugu but the man who translated each sentence into English affected what he imagined was a suitably godlike tone of voice and ended up sounding like a braying ass. This harsh criticism probably reveals how my mind blocked any grace from reaching me: I had gone, not to listen but to find fault.

3

Deccan Setting

Though wretchedly backward earlier, before it gained international prominence thanks to Sathya Sai, Puttaparthi is situated in a fairly dramatic topographical setting. The majesty of the south-west Deccan with its boulder-strewn landscape may not yield much to those who merely scratch its surface, but underneath lies unlimited mineral treasure. In *Paradise Lost*, when Milton speaks of 'the wealth of Ormus and of Ind', he means the spices of Malabar and the gold and jewels of the Deccan. Fabulous riches lie below the austere granite of the peninsular plateau and this provides a happy analogy for Sathya Sai's teaching that within every person lies concealed an untapped treasure. The gurus of the Sai Parampara have appeared on earth to indicate where we need dig to discover that treasure—our own (inner) backyard.

As it happened, the young Sathya Sai first announced that he was Shirdi Sai reborn during a stay with his elder brother at Uravakonda, the site of an old gold mine. Remarkable for its natural temple of raised boulders,

Uravakonda today is a bustling oversized village with brightly painted shops reminiscent of the tiny stone-block house that the young saint lived in. Though loud, the paintwork is tastefully done with attention to detail. As is the case with most of southern India, the people, even when poor, value the satisfaction of doing a thing properly. In the north, loud colours are often allowed to clash and the painting of trucks and bullock carts will often be slapdash. But once south of the Godavari, where the Dravidian script supplants the more angular Devanagari, you'll find that even public conveyances, including the menial rickshaw, are all tricked out with pride and finesse. The headboard on most trucks announces the owner's religious affiliation (Sai Sree Carriers, Sab ka Malik Haulers) and the sides of bullock carts are painted with scenes from the Hindu epics. One can only deduce that the self-respect evidenced in the artistry derives from active devotion to the local gods.

The people of southern Andhra, like the land, are lean but sturdy. The farming community of Rajus into which Sathya Sai was born may be modestly placed in the caste pecking order but, having survived the hardship of tilling the rain-starved red soil, they qualify as the salt of the earth. The salt in their own lives is provided by the natural proprietorship they feel towards the religious myths of the region, re-enacted in countless village dramas conducted in mellifluous Telugu. For centuries, these people have been made to feel like second-class citizens in their own land after the brilliant Kakatiya dynasty was destroyed and supplanted by foreign marauders. Urdu and Marathi were considered the language of the court and polite society respectively while Telugu, despite its

dulcet tone, went into literary decline under the sultanate
of Golconda (which preferred Dakhini Urdu) and was
relegated to the status of a folk tongue. The composer
Thyagraja who made Telugu the language of classical
music could find employment only in Tanjore, a Maratha
fiefdom in Tamil country.

This part of the Deccan, with its pink rock and red
soil, has given rise to the world's richest temple at
Tirupati. It is also the birthplace of modern India's
philosopher–president Dr Radhakrishnan and hosts the
Rishi Valley experimental school set up by another
remarkable Telugu, the philosopher and reluctant saint, J.
Krishnamurti. The crops grown here are marginal, with
millet as the staple. The interior of the Deccan is deprived
of the monsoons, and drought followed by famine has
haunted the region for centuries. With the launch of
Sathya Sai's charitable schemes for drinking water
distribution and irrigation, the prospects for the villagers
here have finally begun to improve. They are now turning
to fruit and vegetable farming and what was once desert
has begun to bloom. The area is fast coming up as India's
vineyard whose grapes are so choice that champagne
produced from them can hardly be distinguished from the
original.

The surroundings of Puttaparthi, overlooked by the
Bukkapatnam hills, were host to one of India's most
famous dynasties in the medieval period. The clue lies in
the name Bukka, which belongs to the younger of the
two brothers who founded the Vijayanagar empire.
Penukonda, one of the capitals of Vijayanagar, is only
thirty-five kilometres from the home of Sathya Sai.
Puttaparthi is graced by the Chitravati flowing through

it; but the river, rising in the lee of the Nandi hills, cannot sustain a flow outside the monsoon. Fortunately for the huge Prasanthi Nilayam ashram that came up on its banks, the river, like the rock of the Deccan, conceals a rich store of largesse underground.

The region of Rayalseema where Puttaparthi is situated (and which echoes exactly the English for 'royal realm') spills west into Karnataka, since the Vijayanagar empire embraced both Telugu and Kannada-speaking areas in the course of the four dynasties which ruled over it. The fabulous capital at Hampi, situated in the magnificently rugged gorge of the Tungabhadra, was the wonder of the medieval world. 'The city is such that the pupil of the eye has never seen anything like it,' remarked Abdul Razzaq, the ambassador to Vijayanagara from the court of Taimur the Lame's son.

Today, Hampi (the local name for Vijayanagar) is in ruins except for the Virupaksha temple, but it is a ruin of such extraordinary majesty and extent that there is nothing to equal it in the world save the Inca capital of Machu Pichhu. For the Sai Parampara, Hampi holds special significance. It was in the Virupaksha temple, under the soaring white gopuram built by the greatest of the Vijayanagar emperors, Krishnadeva Raya, that Sathya Sai, while still a teenager, revealed himself as a miraculous form of Shiva reborn on earth for the sake of his devotees. Since then, Puttaparthi has come to encapsulate the secret of the Deccan and of Sai Baba's nature: outwardly poor, inwardly rich.

The Sai Parampara draws its inspiration from many sources for the good reason that the Deccan, situated halfway between the cultures of the north and south, benefited from the inputs of both. Shirdi in the northern part of the Deccan reflects Aryan influences while Puttaparthi in the southern region has a more Dravidian flavour. Almost uncannily, the linguistic divide between the languages derived from Sanskrit and those belonging to the Dravidian family further south match a dramatic geological divide. The rocks of the Karnataka plateau are ten times older than those of the neighbouring Maharashtra plateau. After years of traversing back and forth between these elusive cultural frontiers, the traveller is none the wiser for this emphatic difference in both mineral and vernacular styles. All he knows is that the south displays more civic awareness and is nominally more life affirming and less fatalistic than the north. Theories abound on why this is so and often, the primary cause is said to be Shankaracharya, the Advaita philosopher whose doctrine of maya, accorded pride of place in mainstream Hinduism, attributes only conditional reality to the world.

It is a widely held belief that Shankaracharya's summing up of the philosophical essence of Hinduism predates the arrival of foreign faiths in India by centuries. But, history suggests the opposite. Both Jews and Christians had a foothold in Kerala soon after the beginning of the Christian era and there are references in the Old Testament to exotic imports from Malabar. A mosque in Kasaragod, in north Kerala, is believed to have been founded in the lifetime of the Prophet, that is to say, almost a century before Shankaracharya was born. Those who are taught to believe that Islam came to north India by the sword are presumably ignorant of its earlier arrival in the south by boat. The later long march of Muhammad bin Tughlaq from Delhi to Daulatabad, turned by popular myth into a mighty exodus, was in fact a failed attempt by the missionary-minded Tughlaq to seed his new capital in the Deccan with model administrators and Sufi mystics who would appeal to the instincts of the common man. The most eminent of Deccan Muslim saints, Hazrat Gesu Daraz, was brought up in Daulatabad. His grave in medieval Gulbarga was so popular that it was accorded the status of a substitute pilgrimage for the haj to Mecca. Banda Nawaz, as the saint is referred to, studied Sanskrit and read the Mahabharata. He was of the opinion that poetry in 'Hindvi' was more inspiring than that written in his native Persian.

The Deccan region has in fact been revolutionary in its theological impact because of the emergence, from its eclectic milieu, of practitioners from the lower end of society's spectrum—shudra saints who stole priestly thunder by their direct devotion to God. Up until the medieval period, Hinduism was unthinkable without a priestly intermediary. Buddhism had challenged this tradition and paid the price. Jainism would survive by trimming its sails to the wind. Undoubtedly, the ingress of egalitarian Islam spurred the idea of direct access to the divine but the Bhakti poets of the Tamil country had stated their preferences two centuries before Islam existed as a religion.

During my first journey through the Deccan hinterland in 1984, I visited Hampi and Bijapur, the medieval capitals of Hindu and Muslim states respectively and, like most tourists, was told how violently antagonistic they were to each other. Now, after half-a-dozen visits to these twin architectural wonders of the Deccan, I have learnt a rather different story. Even a travel writer as astute as Naipaul has swallowed hook, line and sinker the myth that Hampi presented a united Hindu front to the alien sultanates and that it was laid waste by the latter for its defence of the brahminical order. And that Bijapur was an aloof, exclusively Islamic enclave.

A closer study of the period shows that while religious animosities were real, they extended to intra-communal quarrels. Sunni and Shia sultans allied with the Hindu raya against each other, while Lingayat and twice-born (Brahmin) parties at Vijayanagar contested for dynastic superiority. Similarly the Vaishnav philosophy of Ramanuja was pitted against fellow Hindu Advaitists and agnostic Jains. Could it be that the Virupaksha temple and other Shaivite monuments like the Mustard Ganesh survived intact while Vaishnav buildings like the Vitthal temple and the Narasimha monolith were set on fire and vandalized because of sectarian infighting among Hindus? The visitor is always told of Hampi's auspicious beginnings with the blessings of the Sringeri Shankaracharya but never reminded that several regicides marred the reputation of Vijayanagar. Nor is the visitor told that the finest buildings here, like the Lotus Mahal and the Elephant Stables, suggest the hand of Bijapur masons. The evidence points to the opposite of what is popularly believed. Muslims who had a presence in the raya's army may have contributed the finest buildings to the imperial city and though the sultans' armies started the work of ruination, more credit should be given to the weather that made short shrift of the plaster and wooden superstructure that characterized the Hindu architecture.

If I harp on the fusion of Islamic and Hindu inputs in the culture of the Deccan, it is to correct the extant perception in both the north and the south that bitter rivalry between the two was the only reality. It may have been the presiding reality among the rulers but the peasant of the Deccan was too canny not to hedge his bets concerning the welfare of his soul. He may have outwardly confirmed to the orthodoxies of Benares or Mecca, but while responding to spiritual *chamatkar* he would follow his common sense and accept it whether it emanated from a Hindu sanyasi or a Muslim fakir. To gain an understanding of the Sai Baba phenomenon it is crucial to recognize that its popularity derives from the devotee's realization that true religion—love of the soul for its divine originator—is a universal fact of life common to both the Hindu and the Muslim. As a little-known example of how the two faiths could merge in the Deccan we have the remarkable stewardship of certain Bijapur sultans. One called himself 'Jagat Guru' and honoured the goddess Saraswati. Another built what many consider the loveliest building in the Islamic world. The reason why not all in that world are won over by the beauty of the Ibrahim Rauza is that it is the result of Hindu influences. In this rare masterpiece, where the stone reflects the lightness of the spirit, Hinduism's feel for the sinuousness of nature's lines has been breathed into the formal design demanded by Islam.

It was in this eclectic setting that the first Sai Baba emerged in the village of Shirdi in Maharashtra sometime in the late 1850s. No historical details about his origins have been made available so far but mythological speculation to fill the void has reached the proportions of an industry. Despite the dress, speech and behaviour of a

Muslim fakir, the saint's identity has over the years been systematically sought to be reinvented with a brahminical imprimatur by his Hindu followers. More educated disciples who discern in his teaching and demeanour the selfless sign of the true brahmin, now find their speculations brushed aside by crude attempts to manufacture evidence attributing brahmin parentage to Shirdi Sai. Early photos indicate that Shirdi Sai, in contrast to his disciples who are short-statured with the rounded facial features characteristic of the Maratha peasantry, was tall and angular with the high cheekbones reminiscent of Central Asia whence many of the Deccan's Muslim settlers hailed from. These adventurers were known as *Afaqi* and they were the source of much heartburn to the local-born Deccan Muslims who envied their purer Islamic status by virtue of their birth in lands uncontaminated by polytheism.

The Indian tendency to flesh out the bare bones of history with myths makes any study of religious subjects a Holmesian exercise in detection. Myth is not always bad history but can be an edited and inspired résumé wherein licence is taken with minor inaccuracies to present a poetic overview of a complex situation. Keeping the population illiterate and on a diet of legends has its advantages for those in power. While Hindu monarchs relied on court chroniclers and were served by outrageously flattering bards, Deccan sultans sought to make their Islamic credentials more sound by inviting foreign teachers and divines to their court. The racy historian Ferishta hailed from the shores of the Caspian Sea and was not averse to retailing any Deccan folklore favourable to his Islamic party. The origins of some sultanate dynasties—

the result of a usurper's stab in the back—were tarted up and traced to the caliphate rather in the manner of Rajput princes who claimed descent for their ancestors from the sun and moon. The sultan of Bijapur was said by the Muslims to have descended from the caliph of Istanbul while to the Hindu lobby he was the dhobi of a Vaishnav saint in a former life who had been given the boon of being born a sultan the next time round. It was this kind of popular myth that would claim a brahmin parentage for Shirdi Baba just as it invented the spurious notion that the Bahmani muslim dynasty derived its name from the blessings of a brahmin.

Nowhere is religious myth-making more pronounced than in the matter of caste. Here, Hinduism's supposed indifference to history can also be viewed as a strategy to protect its vested interests. Inevitably, when the myth maker is a brahmin, he will insert reminders about the need to look after his community's interests. Unorthodox versions and vernacular renderings rarely get a hearing. The pre-Aryan Shaivite agamic traditions have been largely smothered by Vedic veto, though not entirely. Any evidence unflattering to the Sanskritic ethos tends to be swept under the carpet. Modern India, for example, is asked to believe that Buddhism died a natural death from its ascetic concerns. Evidence suggests, however, that it was shown the door by brahminism, with Buddhist shrines being taken over because of orthodox pressure. The eviction of egalitarian teaching in favour of spiritual elitism (as enunciated by Shankaracharya) is passed off euphemistically as the spoils of religious debate. The acquisitiveness of the twice-born, however, is detectable in the dozens of Hindu shrines and pilgrim centres (such as Ayodhya, Badrinath, Puri, Srisailem, Kanchipuram) which were formerly under Buddhist (or Jain) custodianship.

An example of such myth making is seen in the changes made to the pictures of Shirdi Sai. Some elements have been modified, it seems, to suit Hindu tastes. The early pictures showed him wearing a white *kafni* (gown) and a white bandana knotted at the left. He was usually shown seated on a stone, with his right leg crossed at the knee, placed above his left and his left hand clasping his right foot. This casual, relaxed posture is at odds with the formal yogic asana (pose) used while depicting the orthodox saints. The foot is significant since it represents the classic status of the shudra in the eyes of the orthodox, as viewed in the Vedic depiction of the Purusha (primeval man) wherein 'the brahmin was his mouth . . . of his feet the shudra was born'. At Shirdi's feet lies a pet dog. Dogs are objects of disgust to both orthodox Hindus and Muslims but feature regularly in the unorthodox cults of the Deccan.

It is interesting to note that Sathya Sai, though born with an orthodox Vaishnav name, is viewed as an avatar of the less orthodox Shiva–Shakti form of divinity. However, in the early days of the 'Abode of Well-Being' (as Baba calls his Prasanthi Nilayam spiritual campus), both the unorthodox Agamic and the Sufi content of Shirdi Baba's message appear to have been played down in favour of the Vedic. This latter tradition sees the Sai saints as incarnations of Shiva in his benign Lord of Yogis aspect and not his wilder, unorthodox Pashupatinath form. (Shirdi Baba is accorded the status of Shiva while Sathya Sai is believed to incarnate the powers of both

Shiva and Shakti.) Despite being a less primitive rendering, Shiva-Shakti remains a maverick concept that allows for spontaneity in divine expression. The freedom of spirit that Sathya Sai has reclaimed for the human soul by enshrining the flame of love in it, has resulted in his often embodying the beautiful Ardhanarishvara form of Shiva, a blending in a single body of love's unconquerable yet tender qualities.

Caste plays an important role in the way the genesis of the Sai saints and the legends associated with them have often been portrayed, even though both the saints and the folklore they drew on were inspired by an eclectic mix of Hindu and Muslim, and Aryan and Dravidian influences. Spirituality is so closely interwoven with caste consciousness that any low-born practitioner of the mystical arts automatically finds himself provided with mythological high-caste parentage. The early biographers of the Sai Parampara (all of whom are high-caste males) tend to be defensive about the embarrassing reality of caste. Both the Sai saints have made a point of distancing themselves from its tentacles but the dyed-in-the-wool nature of jati (as caste is referred to in daily life) makes it a problem that refuses to go away.

The injustices inherent in a system of hereditary spiritual status invited early remedy and the monotheistic inroads of Islam and Christianity found a waiting audience in the lower castes groaning under discrimination. This helps explain the anomaly that though the south was shudra territory outside the circle of the twice-born, it managed to achieve much greater literacy than the Aryan heartland. The absence of a brahminical monopoly on learning, together with the introduction of printing presses and vernacular grammars by the missionaries, gave the south a forward-looking outlook that is missing in the north. Today the progressive quality of the Deccan is reflected in the fact that the economies of the southern states are ahead of the north by some fifty years. The capital cities of Bangalore and Hyderabad have achieved in a phenomenally short time-span an international reputation for their success in the information technology sector.

Not surprisingly then, the region south of the Vindhyas has strongly resisted the Sanskritic hegemony of the north despite the inroads it made through colonies of brahmins (known as *agrahara*) who were imported into the region by rulers who wished to be seen as orthodox and possessing a pan-Hindu status. Aryan culture, in the popular affections of the south, seems to have been under constant scrutiny and still is today. It is noticeable, for instance, that while Sathya Sai is open to all regional influences and appreciates the finer points of all cultural expression, the boisterous bhangra of the north comes low on his list of favourites.

Indeed, the resistance to the Sanskritic takeover of the south, even after three thousand years, is still in evidence. The best proof of this is in the (until recently) popular Dravidian movement inspired by the Tamil leader Periyar who was not just violently anti-brahmin but dismissive of all religions. Periyar was a businessman and rationalist who played on popular sentiment that resented northern archetypes such as the depiction of the southern king Ravana as the villain of the Ramayana. In the forty years I have lived in north India, I do not recall reading any in-depth coverage of this Dravidian leader in the national dailies. The silence about Periyar's anti-brahminical discourse is even more deafening than that surrounding Basaveshwara, a medieval poet–statesman who contested the spiritual monopoly of brahmins despite being born a brahmin himself. The interesting fallout of the Dravidian revivalist movement is that it is not as much anti-brahmin as pro-Tamil (the word 'Dravidian' and 'Tamil' are interchangeable). Once the Tamil language was secured against the inroads of Hindi (the child of Sanskrit), the Dravidian movement had no trouble accepting, for instance, brahmin chief ministers of Tamil Nadu.

At the same time, despite the south's championing of its Dravidian character, it is to southern philosophers that orthodox Hinduism owes most of its characteristic teaching. The three great schools—Advaita (monism), Vishistadvaita (conditioned monism) and Dvaita (dualism) are all products of southern minds, viz. Shankaracharya (Kerala), Ramanuja (Tamil Nadu) and Madhava (Karnataka) respectively.

The modern doctrine of Hindutva, based on a chauvinistic, selective use of history emerged from the orthodox milieu of the north Deccan where Tilak and Savarkar argued that the brahminical order was superior to all others. Savarkar's view of Indian society was, like Tilak's, conditioned by the perspective of the privileged and is another example of the feudal ploy that seeks to pass off the opinion of an articulate minority as the national consensus. His theory that all Indians are or were Hindus seems unscientific in view of the fact that India has 4,635 verified distinctive communities. The Deccan was also witness to the plotting of the assassination of Mahatma Gandhi which was hatched in Ahmadnagar.

Savarkar was an accused in the case but was acquitted for lack of evidence. Jawarharlal Nehru had been jailed in the same city during the Quit India movement and his national opus, *The Discovery of India*, was born from this confinement. It is as urbane and open-minded as Savarkar's *Hindutva* (conceived in the Cellular Jail in the Andaman Islands) is communally charged.

Because of its status as a crossroads of sorts, the Deccan provides the full Indian experience as opposed to the slant given by Hindu orthodoxy. In religio-sociological terms, the Deccan illustrates an ongoing contest for spiritual space between the folk wisdom of the peasant and the discredited attempt of a privileged priesthood to hoodwink it with bogus spirituality. So far the Sai Parampara's following appears to be triumphant evidence of how the war is being won. The unorthodox teachers of the Deccan have wrested the universalism of the Upanishads from its orthodox keepers and extended the dignity of this teaching to all levels of society. True freedom—when we are ruled by our inner self—is the Sai Parampara's gift to everyone, irrespective of caste, gender or nation.

{4}

Religious Influences

Today, in every corner of the country, one comes across an increasing number of temples dedicated to the two Deccan saints, Shirdi and Sathya Sai. The immense popularity of the Sai fellowship in modern India can be explained in terms of the lessons learned from the decline of Sanskrit and the rise of the Bhakti movement, the latter also exerting a subtle influence on the manner in which the Sai saints have gone about their mission.

Though Sanskrit learning and culture were prized by the Dravidian rulers and its vocabulary successfully penetrated the derived Dravidian tongues of Malayalam, Telugu and Kannada, Tamil itself—the original inspiration of the Bhakti movement—proved so highly resistant that today it remains India's only living classical language. Sanskrit perished as a spoken tongue from the very refinement it sought to promote. In spite of its scientific structure and resonant beauty, Sanskrit withered from within, its priestly keepers deliberately distancing it from the affairs of everyday life. Language draws life from the roots of the people it serves. By cutting itself off from the common man, any language, no matter how worthy it sounds, dooms itself to mascot status, honoured for its sound rather than its meaning. Sanskrit retains its honorary role but the rise of the Deccan vernaculars—Marathi, Kannada and Telugu, which blossomed under the inspiration of the Bhakti movement—restricted it to an academic means of communication.

Behind the enduring popularity of the Sai phenomenon lies the fact that both the Sai saints shed the aloof orthodoxy that goes with the Sanskritic outlook and shared an urgency to communicate with the masses. While the Sai Parampara may acknowledge the priestly ideal of the brahmin, it contests all automatic claims to spiritual superiority. It has also effectively bypassed the spiritual barrier raised by orthodox Hinduism that without brahminical blessings the pilgrim cannot reach his goal. For Sai Baba every soul is born with the potential to become one with the inner spirit. Unlike Sanskrit, which remained accessible to a privileged few, the Sai Parampara reaches out to all.

This brings us to the Bhakti movement which arose in the south to rejuvenate popular religion and resurrect it from the vain repetition of Vedic rituals to which it had fallen prey. Brahminism's inability to live up to the essential Hindu spirit of inclusiveness had resulted in the implementation of divisive Shastraic law that sapped societal cohesiveness and exposed the subcontinent to foreign monotheistic influences. The student of the medieval battlefield is tempted to conclude that the foreign forces who won despite being vastly outnumbered by Hindu armies were aided by what could be termed surly shudra attitudes. The resentment felt by the lower orders at their exclusion from respectable Hindu society expressed itself in their indifference to the outcome of a battle. A win would make no difference to their predetermined lot while a loss, by embarrassing the rulers, would ease some of their resentment. There is no evidence to suggest that man in medieval India thought in terms of his nation.

The timely rise of theism, in the form of the Bhakti movement, restored buoyancy to a boat internally threatened by the corrosion of caste. At the core of the movement was the philosophy that God could be approached directly through the heart and that priestly intermediaries were redundant. Since the Sai Parampara addresses God in much the same way, and has at its heart rather similar concerns, a look at the dynamics of the Bhakti movement is in order.

At the centre of unorthodox Shaivite Bhakti was Basaveshwara, a Deccan brahmin who in the twelfth century repudiated his ancestral faith and founded a casteless creed popularly known as Lingayat or Virasaiva. Orthodoxy had good reason to be chary of Basaveshwara's movement since it appears to have its roots in tantric sects which popularly are imagined to pamper society's lower passions. At least this was the view put out by philosopher–pamphleteers like Ramanuja who, because they felt their power base threatened, resorted to exaggeration. Worse still, the spiritual preceptor of the lapsed brahmin was an untouchable.

Basaveshwara has been shunned for centuries by the orthodox as outside the pale of Hinduism for his audacity in not just preaching but practising the doctrine of love for, and direct communion with Shiva. But he saw

himself as a true Hindu and orthodox brahminism as the
pretender. His inspiration was not the imported Vedas
but the Agamic lore of the south. The single-minded
devotion and zeal to serve the 'Lord of the Meeting
Rivers' (as Basaveshwara addressed Shiva in his profound
and pithy verse) prompted the later Muslim rulers of the
Deccan to conclude that the Lingayats were monotheists.
To bring matters to a head, Basavanna (as he was known
before his deification) promoted inter-caste marriage—
something still unthinkable to India's uneducated villager—
and encouraged the education of women. Criminally,
according to the code of his day, he filled the minds of
the untouchables with spiritual ideas above their station,
unforgivably threatening the pillar on which orthodox
society rested. He refused the sacred thread of the twice-
born to demonstrate that real religion cannot be physically
inherited but has to be cultivated by devotion.

After the noble universalism of the Upanishads,
Hinduism had to wait nearly two millennia for the
theistic teachings of the Maharashtrian saints to reach the
same level of spiritual excellence. The great literary saint
Jnanesvar, though born a brahmin, adopted unorthodox
habits and showed sympathy for Guru Gorakhnath's
teachings. Gorakhnath is another of the shadowy
archetypal yogis who looms large in public affection in
the Deccan for his liberated views on what a man may
eat and drink in his quest for God. Jnanesvar is famous
for making a buffalo recite the Vedas in order to ridicule
the claims of the orthodox priests. What this story may
symbolize is that the latter, who considered the shudras
little better than beasts, now had to come to terms with
the Bhakti movement whose saints were men and women

with ordinary occupations, not born to teach religion. Namdev, a contemporary of Jnanesvar, was the son of a tailor (though tradition has left scope for invention by claiming he was found as a baby floating in the river at Pandharpur). The pilgrim place of Pandharpur in southern Maharashtra, dedicated to several shudra literary saints, has a special significance since it reveals not just the human face of Hinduism but is also an assertion of the common man's right to direct access to divinity. Another great saint of the Maratha country was Tukaram, an impoverished shopkeeper with a shining faith in Vitthal, which powered all his compositions. Orthodoxy punished his presumption by forcing him to throw his verses into the river. In keeping with Bhakti traditions, Vitthal is a rustic Marathi rendering of Vishnu. He stands informally with arms akimbo at Pandharpur, a peasant variant on the theme of the Brindaban lover. His consort is not the romantic mistress figure of Radha Rani but a homely no-nonsense character who represents the enduring relationship that the mundane state of marriage symbolizes. Above all, these unsophisticated but reassuring figures of a divinized peasant farmer and his wife are accessible to every devotee irrespective of caste.

Maharashtrian folklore is also replete with the numinous figure of Dattatreya who seems to perform the role of bridging Aryan orthodoxy with Deccan folk religion. He is considered the inspiration behind the Mahanubhava sect of Vaishnavites, remarkable for holding several unorthodox beliefs and practices. Dattatreya is often depicted holding four dogs on a leash. The orthodox interpret this as his mastery of the four Vedas; the unorthodox see it as the reining in of Vedic influences. So

popular is Dattatreya in the Deccan that opposing schools
of Bhakti and Advaita have arisen in his name. Thursday
(dedicated to the guru) is set aside as Dattatreya's weekly
day of worship.

An equally egalitarian outlook which remains aloof
from any priestly involvement is the hallmark of both
Shirdi Baba's and Sai Baba's philosophy. Guruvar or
Thursday is observed as their sacred day and Sai Baba
like Shirdi Baba before him, dotes on his dogs. Early
devotees claim that often, when they had their photographs
taken with Sathya Sai, the developed print would depict
him in the form of Dattatreya. In recent years, a Dattatreya
shrine has come up in Puttaparthi near the samadhi of
Sathya Sai's mother. That Sathya Sai Baba is well aware
of these popular religious movements is clear from the
famous occasion in 1958 when he materialized a copy of
the Bhagavad Gita from a riverbed and presented it to the
eminent scientist Dr Bhagavantam. On this occasion,
recognizing the figures represented on a badge worn by a
devotee, he announced that it was the couple Kusum-
Haranath who had given a fillip to the Namasankirtan
movement in modern Bengal. Namsmarana, the practice
of reciting God's name, was common to all Bhakti
schools and it is practised by many devotees in Puttaparthi.

*

The *vibhuti abishek* that marks the climax of the Sathya
Sai spiritual calendar at Shivratri not only takes the
student back to the *dhuni* of the Shirdi fakir, but beyond
to the unorthodox figures who have influenced religion in
the Deccan: Gorakhnath, Dattatreya and Basaveshwara.

The *lingodbhava leela* (Sathya Sai's materializing from his person one or more shivalingams) that follows the vibhuti outpouring is a highly unorthodox rite suggestive of both the Lingayat loyalty to the outward symbol of Shiva, as well as those cults which worship Shiva as pure energy. There are two levels in operation here, the exoteric and esoteric. In the person of Sathya Sai Baba it is believed Shiva is paired with Parvati, the orthodox wifely consort and/or Shakti, the unpredictable feminine force. There are thus two readings of the lives of the Deccan saints and, while scholars argue over which is historically and theologically correct, the devotee (practising the Sai teaching of placing love above all else) allows his feelings to get the better of logic and accepts both versions.

More sophisticated devotees of Shirdi Sai Baba like 'Hemadpant' Dabholkar and Kaka Dixit made a conscious effort to overcome their orthodox brahminical distaste for Muslim habits. Dixit, always quick on the uptake as befitted an eminent lawyer, had learned that Shirdi Sai felt actual physical pain if anyone insulted the sentiments of those belonging to other religions. He realized that the easiest way to please Baba was to behave generously to the outnumbered Muslim devotees. It was his legal acumen, at the passing of the saint, which headed off a likely ugly showdown between devotees of opposing religions. The undercurrent of Hindu–Muslim tensions in the recorded life of Shirdi Baba is sought to be played down but was so real that it resulted in Baba's ashram being attached by the government to prevent further friction after the saint's demise. Hemadpant, while openly acknowledging the Hindu takeover of a Muslim festival at Shirdi, states that the transition was followed by 'no outbreak of any riots worth the name', thus admitting that the majority imposition had upset the minority. Another instance showing how the minority did not take kindly to the takeover of their pir can be detected in the words of the orthodox biographer Narasimhaswami, who, after reporting the aggressive resistance of local Muslim devotees to the applying of sandalwood paste on Shirdi Baba's forehead, notes that aggression was met with aggression and 'the Muslims were cowed down'. An obvious example of Narasimhaswami's policy of Hinduization can be seen in his *Guide to Shirdi* (1947) where a picture of Shirdi Baba in his traditional seated pose as a Muslim fakir is followed by a photo of the author holding his modified version of the same picture with deities from the Hindu pantheon superimposed around the garlanded saint.

From this denial of all that Shirdi Sai stood for and the apparent obsessive concern to appropriate his Islamic heritage, it might seem that the saint's teaching of the underlying unity of religions failed to find a hold even in the streets of the village where he spent sixty years of his life. Ironically, given his attempts to get Hindus to rise above issues of caste and Muslims to overcome their narrow vision of the Godhead, the official life of Shirdi Baba continues to be published by a committee appointed by a court receiver. It is hardly surprising that the high-caste biographers of Shirdi Sai committed to foisting brahminical parentage on him have carefully re-edited the physical evidence of his actually belonging to a Sufi order in the Nizam's domain. His uncoloured Sufi robe now appears dyed *gerua* (saffron) after the fashion of Hindu sanyasis; his favourite dog Manohar is missing in the calendar art portraits; his trimmed upper lip, denoting Muslim practice, is now provided with a Hindu householder's moustache; and his tattered clothing is replaced with the immaculate dry-cleaned raiment befitting a master of wisdom in the eyes of middle-class Indians. (In 2002, Sathya Sai had a larger than life-size figure of Shirdi Sai—whom he refers to as his 'former body'— raised in his Puttaparthi outdoor stadium. This stands clothed in the original white. However, the prayer hall of Sathya Sai currently displays a full-length portrait of Shirdi Sai wearing the saffron colours of renunciation.)

Ultimately, what is more important than arguing if his lip was shaved like a Muslim's or mustachioed like a Hindu's is to record the electrifying impact he had on his contemporaries, whatever their religious upbringing and the influence he continues to exert on his devotees today. To leave the matter there would serve the genuine interests of those who feel such disputes are best ignored. Unfortunately, it would also serve the interests of those who seek to manipulate the public mind and pass off myth as history. Modern India is being led up the garden path by these deliberate distorters of the nation's traditional pluralism. Since the Sai message is opposed to the religious divide which these lobbies seek to widen, it is worthwhile to examine in some detail how devotional ingenuity can successfully mislead one, through a series of apparently innocent concoctions, to accept myth as fact.

The fact is that we still do not know Shirdi's physical origins, whatever mythology may seek to embroider into his past. We owe the origin of the story that Shirdi Sai had brahmin parents to Mahlsapathy. He was Baba's very first disciple, being a resident of Shirdi and the custodian of the village temple dedicated to Khandoba, one of the more primitive deities of Maharashtra. Immediately on his arrival in the village, Shirdi Baba, in the dress of a fakir, expressed his pleasure at the peace surrounding Mahlsapathy's temple and spoke of his desire to settle nearby. The custodian, a simple villager who had been brought up to believe that all Muslims are iconoclasts, was aghast at the suggestion and brusquely redirected the fakir to the tumbledown mud-walled mosque. To his surprise, the fakir was not offended and went peacefully. To Mahlsapathy's greater surprise, the fakir began referring to his adopted mosque as 'Dwarkamai' after the Hindu place of pilgrimage. Soon, Shirdi Baba's detached bearing had such a calming effect on the priest that he found he could not tear himself away from the fakir's presence. Mahlsapathy was drawn to the mosque, a place all his orthodox instincts abhorred.

The biographer Hemadpant mentions the details of Baba's birth as a confidence which was privately shared with him by Mahlsapathy who presumably got this information from Baba himself. Nobody else was made privy to this information and it seems strange that it should have been vouchsafed after a lifetime of emphatic refusal on the part of the saint to attach any importance to such matters. Indeed, it ran counter to the fakir's teachings. One explanation could be that the information confided was meant to be taken symbolically and the hearer accepted it as literal fact. Two questions, however, remain unanswered. Why should Mahlsapathy share a private confidence with Hemadpant? And why should Hemadpant, who had promised Shirdi Baba not to include any controversial matter as a condition for writing his biography, print this and other disputable hearsay? Since, by all accounts, Shirdi Baba was coherent until his passing, we can only question the motives of Mahlsapathy. Narasimhaswami in his *Life of Sai Baba* (1955) ingenuously argues that the priest's integrity cannot be doubted but overlooks the fact that it was the same priest's prejudice that caused Shirdi Baba to make his abode in a mosque.

The suspicion that the less educated devotees might have been encouraged to echo the wishful thinking of the educated lobby is strengthened by the account of the next witness, Das Ganu Maharaj. A police constable who had failed to achieve his ambition of becoming a sub-inspector, Das Ganu Maharaj was gifted with the Deccan peasant's talent for poetry. To offset his inventive genius was a fanatical loyalty to the Hindu cause which led him, in spite of Shirdi Baba's blessings, to choose a brahmin guru. Das Ganu's genius extended to 'researching' some two hundred kilometres downstream of Shirdi and coming up, at the village of Pathri, with a melodramatic scenario according to which a pious brahmin couple abandon their newborn baby who is found and adopted by a benevolent zamindar of nearby Selu. This zamindar who 'protects Hindus from Muslims' turns out to be none other than Venkusa, the supposed teacher of Shirdi Baba. Since Das Ganu Maharaj specialized in a school of Marathi verse famous for its overblown (and, according to Narasimhaswami, lewd and obscene) style, it is hardly surprising that there has been no credible confirmation of either location or personages to back up this inspired research. In view of their known prejudices, Mahlsapathy's and Das Ganu Maharaj's claims to confidences from

Shirdi Baba cannot constitute unflawed evidence. Of course, Das Ganu Maharaj's motive was love and—from his point of view—he was bestowing an honour on the fakir. The seeds sown by the village bard have now borne devotional fruit of such intense fervour that there is no way historical evidence—even if there were any—could turn the clock back.

The chauvinistic Das Ganu Maharaj was the first to overtly brahminize Shirdi Baba by his attempt to give a Hindu identity to Baba's mysterious guru Venkusa. Narasimhaswami mentions how, when the zamindar of Selu visited Suvag Shah's tomb in Ahmedabad, he was told that he had been Kabir's guru in a former life and was destined to be so once more (since Shirdi Baba is also viewed by some as Kabir come again). Thus, there are both Hindu and Muslim elements to the tale of the mysterious guru which Das Ganu Maharaj is either ignorant of or (more likely) hostile to. Narasimhaswami, being an orthodox Hindu from the Tamil country, is sympathetic to the theory that the name 'Venkusa' was derived from the deity at Tirupati, completely ignoring the fact that the latter part of the word 'sa' is the popular pronunciation of 'Shah', the surname that is sometimes attached to Sufi pirs. Illustrating how regional loyalties can affect the interpretation of evidence, Narasimhaswami concludes that Shirdi Baba is actually Lord Venkateshwara of Tirupati.

But could it be that Venkusa is actually a garbled form of 'Fakir Shah', the Sufi equivalent of Dattatreya, and honoured in popular affections throughout the Deccan? According to H.V. Sathe, a government officer who was a disciple of Shirdi Sai, he often heard Shirdi

Baba use the word 'Shah' after the name of his pir, which others identified as 'Roshan Shah' ('Lord of light'). Ra Ganapati, the learned Tamil author of *Baba Satya Sai*, notes that the historical Fakir Shah, honoured by all Deccan Sufis, lived two hundred years before the time of Shirdi Baba and his *pirsthan* at Mirzgaon was known for its powerful 'psychic vibrations'. Ra Ganapati further notes that Datta Baba and Fakir Shah are probably the same.

Vishwas Kher and M.V. Kamath, in *Sai Baba of Shirdi: A Unique Saint* (1991), mention that 'Shah Fakir' is the Muslim version of a Hindu deity sponsored by the medieval saint of the Dattatreya order, Narasimha Saraswati. Also known as 'Shahdutta Allama Prabhu', this figure not only merged Hindu and Muslim streams of devotion, but actually flirted with the unthinkable notion of finding divinity in an untouchable. Allama Prabhu is none other than Basaveshwara's outcaste teacher, a brilliant mystical poet against whom a disdainful orthodoxy has maintained a conspiracy of silence for seven centuries. His writings have only now found a respectable audience in A.K. Ramanujan's *Speaking of Shiva*. Till today, Lingayat *jangamas* are accorded honour in Islamic festivals in the Deccan. As further evidence of the combined Hindu–Muslim experiment in devotion, in his study on tantra, the Austrian scholar–sanyasi Aghehananda Bharati names a Dattatreya temple near Chikmagalur in the Western Ghats where a Sufi fakir read the rubric in garbled Urdu and Sanskrit. A few years ago, this temple's green Sufi flag was hauled down by activists and the saffron flag of Hindutva run up. This in turn has caused the modern followers of Basaveshwara to rally against the illiberal policies of the Hindu establishment. The age-old conflict between the politico-spiritual agenda of Aryavartha (the land of the noble) and the Deccan instinct to resist the colonization of its soul continues.

Kher has been a trustee of the Sri Sai Baba Sansthan of Shirdi and has examined the genealogies of the Pathri brahmin families. On the slender clue that a certain family 'has produced persons of higher urges and impulses' he has followed his own impulse to conclude that one of their progeny must have been Shirdi Baba. Following from his findings (and cynics will say explaining their motivation), he purchased land from the said family in 1994 and raised a *janmabhumi* (birthplace) temple.

To complicate the picture of Shirdi Baba's presumed Islamic identity, we have several instances where Sathya Sai Baba himself has confirmed—in public—his Hindu beginnings in the Shirdi incarnation as the son of a brahmin boatman in Pathri. In *Sathyam, Sivam, Sundaram* the official biography of the Puttaparthi saint, Prof. Kasturi writes that Sathya Sai Baba first elaborated on his Pathri beginnings to two of his former village school teachers, one of whom rendered Baba's recollections into Telugu verse in 1944. Since Sathya Sai goes into considerable detail and even gives the date of his birth in 1835, the student of history is lured further into a cul-de-sac. Sathya Sai apparently does not accept the versions of Das Ganu and Narasimhaswami entirely but confirms the *Shri Sai Satcharita* of Hemadpant as canonical. Kher also accepts Hemadpant as a more reliable source of information. Dr Gokak, the distinguished Kannada litterateur, in his biography *Bhagavan Sri Sathya Sai*

Baba (1975), puts the question of Shirdi Baba's early life to Sathya Sai who then elaborates on the Pathri beginnings but more, it seems, in a mythological tone than historical (The Indian ear delights in matching sounds and 'Parthi'— short for Puttaparthi—goes well with Pathri). The students who comprised the audience were presumably expected to visualize the essence of Baba's words and not view them as details from a gazetteer. That would help elide the question of why a pious mother should abandon in haste her newborn son whom she knew to be of divine origin. Gokak gets over this awkward situation with the words 'her duty lay in that direction', while to Kasturi falls the task of spelling out an embarrassing contradiction: 'So full of the spirit of renunciation were the parents that they left the newborn babe (an incarnation of Shiva) to the protection of the angels of the forest.'

The most reliable account of Shirdi Baba's life in English to date is Antonio Rigopoulos's meticulously researched *The Life and Teachings of Sai Baba of Shirdi* (1993) in which the author balances scholarship with sympathy, and caution with charity. He is impressed not just by the wealth of detail Sathya Sai provides about Pathri but by its authenticity. (However, the author apparently is not fluent in any of the Deccan languages.) Whatever be the lack of scientific method in such research, the fact is that Pathri has now been put on the folklore and economic map after almost a century of incremental mythologizing. This will be seen by some as the ongoing leela of the fakir.

Perhaps the reason for strengthening the Hindu origins over the Islamic is the pragmatic acceptance that the mass of Sathya Sai's following is of the former persuasion and it makes sense to address them in the medium with which they are familiar. Mythology, until very recent times, was viewed by Western intellectuals as crude and unreliable folk memory open to distortion and manipulation by its pundit retailers. Thanks to the Jungian school of psychology, the virtues of myth have been rescued and, like dream interpretation, restored to a respectable place in the repertory of human responses to psychic promptings. In weaving the Hindu beginnings of Shirdi Baba, Sathya Sai is not asserting the Hindutva creed of Savarkar that all Indian minorities should accept that they are subsumed Hindus. By connecting Shirdi Sai's inner lineage to Hindu mythology, Sathya Sai is able to bring out the underlying energy that both figures have been able to tap, namely the shakti of Shiva, the first of Hindu gods and the most compassionate when it comes to his disciples' welfare. Chronologically, the revelation of Islam came later and Shirdi Baba consistently demonstrated that he accepted the underlying oneness of Hindu and Muslim perceptions of divinity. Whether compassion was revealed in the form of Shiva or in the merciful figure of Allah made no difference to him: his fakir and the world's malik (owner) were one and the same. His life was dedicated to underlining this oneness and identifying it as a compassion that transcended all labels.

Sathya Sai's details of Shirdi Sai's Pathri beginnings may therefore be symbolic in indicating a common source of divine energy that predates the formal message of Islam but not the ever-present reality of Allah. This, in the Hindu dress of Andhra, is perceived most dynamically in the Shiva–Parvati canon of mythology which provides a rich mine of spiritual reference instantly recognizable to the bulk of Sathya Sai followers. Hence, many identified Sathya Sai Baba as the embodiment of the benevolent aspect of Shiva while the more crotchety aspect of the Great Yogi could be likened to the mad fakir of Shirdi. It is instructive here to recall the advice Gurdjieff gave to his students, that they must take all of their teacher's words *seriously* but not literally. The student of grace can avail of mythology's magic carpet to waft his concern back to non-physical essentials. Compared to the love the mere thought of Shirdi Baba arouses in devotees, the grubbing for the details of his corporeal arrival in this world seems inconsequential.

{5}

The Remarkable Fakir of Shirdi

I first visited Shirdi in 1984 on my way back to Delhi from Puttaparthi by bus. My budget for the whole journey was Rs 500. The itinerary went so smoothly and the passage through the interior of the Deccan was so pleasant that I could only put it down to some grace at work.

I arrived late at Pune and hoped to stay the night at Rajneesh's ashram which was then much in the news for the outspokenness of its guru. However, I was rebuffed and given the impression that only cash-rich foreigners were welcome at the ashram gates. This would turn out to be a blessing in disguise. I decided to catch a late-night bus to Shirdi and, though I only reached there in the early hours of the morning, the welcome was so sincere and warm that I immediately realized this was the home of genuine religion whereas the Pune ashram only seemed to affect a religious air. In defence of the latter, though, I might add that Mirtola enjoyed a similar reputation for standoffishness. Both these ashrams catered to those who considered themselves advanced students and, unlike Sai

Baba's organization, were not geared to accept every new arrival at their gates.

Fundamental to the Sai Parampara is the intensely personal relationship that holds between guru and shishya. So devoted was Shirdi Baba to his shishyas that he invariably appeared to them in their hour of need. Likewise astral visitations have been vouched for over the years by thousands of Sai devotees, convinced of the master's presence at their abode no matter how far from Shirdi or Puttaparthi.

Any study of the psychic realm and its remarkable energies is bound to be a vexed undertaking. Those who are born with this extra dimension learn to be careful who they reveal its powers to. It is also important to remember that such deployment of psychic energy is done not so much to impress the devotees as to console them in times of distress. These journeys are compassionate excursions in answer to prayer. And the prayer being answered could have come from someone unaware of Shirdi Baba's existence. One example—used by Arthur Osborne to conclude his book on Shirdi Baba (*The Incredible Sai Baba*, 1957)—includes all the ingredients that are typical of the thousands of instances reported. I can vouch for its accuracy to some extent. I had arrived in Calcutta to teach in the school of which Osborne was the principal. One of Osborne's neighbours in the apartment block he lived in was an old lady who had been a Catholic nun but who, after a midlife spiritual crisis, had decided to quit the order, a brave but foolhardy decision. Only then did she realize that she did not have the qualifications or training for a job nor even a place to go to. As she sat in her cell plunged in despair, to her utter astonishment, a tall fakir in white appeared and told her not to worry about the future. It had been taken care of. (She was now more worried about how a man had managed to enter the nunnery!) Unperturbed, the fakir demanded a certain amount of money as dakshina, which she said she did not possess. He reminded her that she kept a small amount locked in her cupboard. She recalled then that she did have some money but had forgotten about it. When she went to the cupboard to retrieve it, the kindly visitor disappeared as suddenly as he had come. Events conspired to prove the fakir right. A compassionate nephew welcomed her into his Calcutta flat next to Osborne's and, in thanksgiving, the aunt would go to early-morning mass daily to bless her mysterious visitor. On hearing the description of the fakir, Osborne told her he could guess who her visitor was. He produced a photograph of Shirdi Baba whom the ex-nun immediately recognized as her deliverer.

*

The lives of both Shirdi and Sathya Sai have been sought to be Sanskritized by the pens of well-meaning authors who imagine that they are doing society a favour by editing out facts like the fondness the surrounding populations of both Shirdi and Puttaparthi have for meat and country liquor. The point these fastidious pens miss is that true religion has little to do with what a man eats or drinks. In sanitizing the guru they have overlooked the spiritual hardiness of the shishyas who, in spite of their worldly appetites, can still recognize the real spirit when they see it. Shirdi Sai and Sathya Sai have been 'made' not by the pens of the fastidious but by the living faith of earthy peasants.

We are told that the fakir first came to the village around the late 1850s when he was only sixteen and returned three years later to spend the rest of his days in Shirdi, not leaving his mosque residence (except for a few months when he moved to a nearby village to take lessons from a maulana) until summoned by the Fakir above in 1918. His fame for producing psychic phenomena was not widely known outside Shirdi until 1892. Hemadpant started visiting the saint only in 1910. As such, most of what he writes is based on tradition plus all the inventiveness that fifty years of silence and hindsight can stimulate.

The details of the Shirdi fakir's life and teachings, whether provided by Hemadpant or Narasimhaswami or Das Ganu Maharaj, are rather random, somewhat subjective and prone to mythical embellishment. We have already seen the attempt to adorn Shirdi Sai with brahmin parentage and the crusading zeal with which these high-caste biographers sought to make the fakir fit in with their Hindu notions of a saint. These authors reflect the orthodox Hindu viewpoint which feels beleaguered in the modern age by the fact that the monotheistic religions have a solid, verifiable basis in history. The popular theory that Shirdi Baba had been born of brahmin parents (who then abandoned him) and was later adopted by a fakir, though subtly contrived to satisfy a believer, raises to the student of history as many questions as it answers. Since no concrete data is referred to and the subject is highly disputable in historical terms, the reader is confused—until he understands the biographers' motives.

The success of these tactics is clear when we find the normally cautious Arthur Osborne stating that it is 'fairly certain' that Baba's parents were brahmins. Even stranger, in the absence of any evidence, is Osborne's assertion that the parents were 'middle class'. The fact that Shirdi Baba's ears were pierced (a common feature of some Sufi orders) is taken to be proof of brahmin parentage, but if you go by the myth that he was abandoned at the moment of birth, the question of piercing by his parents could not arise. Quite apart from societal abhorrence at the abandonment of (male) infants, the crucial qualification for brahminical status is guarantee of birth from a brahmin. The parental religion of a newborn waif can only be guessed at. However, abandonment at birth would conveniently allow scope for the rite of circumcision—the mark that sets the monotheist apart from the Hindu—to be effected should this be necessary to tally with later biographical requirements. Then the child's adoption by a fakir could be used to 'explain' possession of an outward monotheistic signifier. This situation has not arisen since no life of the saint from a Muslim perspective has yet been published. Forever annoyed at his disciples' preoccupation with caste, Hemadpant records that one day the old saint appeared naked before his followers. Since none of the Hindu biographers tell us what they saw, one may presume that whatever it was did not ease their concerns about his brahmin pedigree. Hemadpant does however confess that Shirdi Baba approved of the rite of circumcision. The only evidence published so far to suggest that the fakir was not circumcised stems—as does the saint's supposed boast of high-caste birth—from a single unverified high-caste source.

Howard Murphet, a journalist rather than a historian, is more cautious in saying that Shirdi Sai was 'somehow' adopted by a Muslim, while Vishwas Kher and M.V. Kamath are convinced that the guru was a Sufi. (Their best-selling biography begins as a balanced and wide-ranging account of the life of the saint but disappoints when it diverts to publicizing Kher's theory that he had discovered, in 1976, the actual brahmin homestead of Shirdi Baba in Pathri.) Professor Charles White suggests that Shirdi Sai was the disciple of both a Muslim as well as a Hindu guru. He argues that in the last days of his life the old fakir wanted only brahmins at his bedside and that this supports the case for Shirdi's own high-caste birth. But White may be taking the word 'brahmin' too literally. When Shirdi Baba spoke about his mosque being a place for 'white brahmins', he might have been teaching through allegory and referring to a quality of soul found in the sincere follower of any religion.

In this tussle between competing claims one tends to overlook the fact that Shirdi Baba did in fact triumph over concerns of caste and religiosity. The best example is Hemadpant who writes with a remarkable open-mindedness about aspects of the fakir's lifestyle (such as cooking meat biryani and smoking the chillum) that would have disgusted his brahminical notions of what constitutes spiritual hygiene. In spite of these glaring affronts, his attraction to what the fakir had to teach him was strong enough for him to ignore them. Often the teacher would taunt him and other high-caste devotees about their inherited prejudices and, at the same time, jeer at and turn away any Muslim visitor who paraded his superior spiritual status, such as having performed the Haj to Mecca.

According to some, in the early days Shirdi Baba wore a codpiece, practised hatha yoga and loved to wrestle. Once on being worsted in combat he gave up the athletic mode and began wearing his well-known, torn white kafni, the dress adopted by Muslim fakirs. He rarely performed namaz in the orthodox manner. Opinions about his knowledge of the Koran are diametrically opposed. Hindus claim he needed instruction, while Abdul, a close Muslim follower, insisted he could quote Koranic suras by heart. Every day, throughout his life, he begged for food, going from door to door, even after he had become famous. He appeared to be a law unto himself and the public could not make up its mind whether he was genuinely inspired or just plain cracked. Unconcerned about what people thought, his behaviour remained eccentric and his language could often be abusive. He spent much of the time carrying water from a well to maintain a small garden. Until he won regard for his spiritual prowess from outsiders, the local people of Shirdi regarded him as a harmless lunatic at whom the village children were accustomed to throw stones.

Altogether unpredictable, the Shirdi fakir could greet visitors with foul abuse or gentle address. These extremes of soft-hearted benevolence and violent censure ensured that only those who were serious in their search survived the spiritual roulette he played. Like Gurdjieff, he taught in riddles, provoking and sometimes shocking his visitors by demanding money. Both could be withering with people who displayed spiritual airs and both loved to deflate claims to holiness. With the rich they could be offensive but with the poor they were charitable, taking on hopeless cases to demonstrate that love can conquer everything. Shirdi Baba appointed Bhagoji, a faithful servant who suffered from leprosy, to bear his processional parasol (the sign of royalty in the Deccan). Unable to shake off his orthodox conditioning, Hemadpant gratuitously attributes Bhagoji's leprosy to the fact that he must have been a sinner in a former life.

The fakir kept earthen lamps filled with oil burning in the mosque, giving a very Hindu touch to his devotions. It was the miraculous conversion of water into oil by him—after the manner of Christ turning water into wine in Cana—that propelled Shirdi Baba to saintly status in religious folklore. (Rustic audiences all over the world respond more readily to divine gifts when they come with economic benefits.) He also kept a narrow plank tenuously suspended some six feet above the floor on which it was assumed he rested at night. But how could he reach this rickety contraption on which oil lamps were also kept burning? Some see it as symbolic of his siddhi that he required little sleep and instead visited his disciples in an out-of-the-body state.

The chief visible mark of the fakir's religious sadhana was to tend the sacred fire (dhuni) in his tumbledown mosque, where he would squat puffing, after the manner of holy men, on his chillum, discussing the nature of God. Later, when he became famous, the ash (udi) from this fire would become a great healing agent believed to possess the spiritual power he had amassed during his years of penance. He also liked to sing (in Arabic, according to some) and loved the religious processions that were a part of village festivals. He had arrived in Shirdi with a marriage barat and this might be considered unusual behaviour for a holy man but what made him different from a million other similar sadhu figures all over the subcontinent was the sense of authority that marked his words. Usually, wandering mendicants pick up a smattering of spiritual knowledge and retail it to their village hosts in return for a night's hospitality. Baba's words, however, were authentic and his presence attractive. Even those like Mahlsapathy, the village priest who harboured intense distaste for Muslims, found themselves inexorably drawn by Shirdi Baba's aura.

Hemadpant understood the significance of Shirdi Baba as a bridge between Hindus and Muslims. There was not just mistrust but active disgust between the two communities, each resting on its pride in the nature of its own spirituality. Shirdi lay in the hinterland of Maharashtra where the descendants of Shivaji contested the spiritual space bordering the dominions of the Nizam. The Sufis were traditionally healers of the communal discord that afflicted every village. Their brand of Islam had been enlarged by Hindu insights on the nature of the divine and Shirdi Baba was the perfect example of how it was possible to draw on the best of both faiths to arrive at a universal religion.

This teaching of the underlying oneness of all religions was not a theoretical nicety with Shirdi Baba but a driving concern. He would get physically ill if he heard any religion abused. He would agonize and lose his temper over the petty communal one-upmanship of his followers, both Hindu and Muslim, and try and make them see how they betrayed not only their religion but themselves in refusing to see the essential similarity of their opposing points of view. It is a testimony to the tenacity of inherited attitudes that all three biographers

Hemadpant, Narasimhaswami and later Kasturi (on Sathya Sai) fall short of projecting their subjects as spiritual forces that belong to mankind. They seem content to portray them not just as embodiments of Hindu ideals (which is understandable) but as ideal Hindus (which seems to underestimate both their appeal and message).

Sri Purohit Swami mentions in his spiritual autobiography how on his visit to meet the Shirdi saint, the greatest miracle he witnessed was Shirdi Baba's complete and steadfast composure. As if echoing the teaching of Shirdi Baba, he concludes that the spiritual goal 'is established in men's hearts and not outwardly to dazzle the eye'. At the root of such composure is compassion towards all living beings, the keynote of the Sai Parampara teaching which is exemplified with startling clarity in the way Shirdi Baba sometimes ate, allowing dogs and birds to share his meal. To the orthodox this was the most disgusting of habits and Shirdi Baba would push them further by suggesting they eat forbidden items like onion or even mutton which he cooked regularly. In the last few years, it seems the process went into reverse and the disciples influenced the teacher's habits. Shirdi Baba became more accommodating of his many Hindu followers' tastes. There are several instances of Baba teaching by giving examples of lower forms of life which most of us take for granted and attach no spiritual significance to. Thus, on occasion he would accuse a disciple of striking him and when the astonished devotee pleaded innocent, he would be told that the dog chased away by the devotee in anger was Baba himself. Shirdi Baba would extend the argument to ants and when a devotee complained that Baba had not eaten the food he cooked for him, he was told that it had been eaten by Baba in his ant-form! Humour abounds in Shirdi Baba's down-to-earth teaching in Marathi but most of it gets diluted in translation.

There was one other thing the guru was adamant about, and that was avoiding any controversial debates over religion or criticizing other gurus or spiritual paths. Before he allowed Hemadpant to write his biography, he insisted that no hard-and-fast opinions of the author should be expressed nor should he refute the opinions of anyone else. Only when Hemadpant agreed to these conditions was the project blessed. For centuries, India has suffered from acrimonious religious debate and it is important to realize that often theological exchanges lead nowhere. While such arguments may theorize about God, they do not add a cubit to a man's understanding of his own soul. Baba's appeal was directed at the heart of the devotee.

Shirdi Baba passed away in 1918 under circumstances that reminded many of the departure of the mystic poet Kabir from the world in 1518. This Muslim weaver so deeply stirred Hindu feelings for 'simple union' with God through bhakti that, like his spiritual descendant Shirdi Sai, Kabir was 'awarded' a brahmin mother to ensure that at least in spiritual lore if not in actual life his inspiration had a 'proper' source. As with Shirdi Sai on his deathbed, there were altercations between the two sets of Kabir's followers, Hindu and Muslim. The story goes that when a settlement had been reached, the litigants, to their surprise, found heaps of fragrant garlands but no body. On Shirdi Baba's departure, instead of flowers there was a more prosaic court order that restrained the claims of both parties.

6

Exalting Those of Low Estate

What is unique about Puttaparthi and sets it apart from other janmabhumi sites like Bethlehem, Ayodhya, or Lumbini is that you can see the actual physical location of the birth of a spiritual master. Rarely in history has the student of grace been gifted with an opportunity to watch the divine at work from the ringside. Over the last sixty years, the observer has been able to witness the unfolding of the extraordinary ordinariness of life's spiritual dimension operating in the daily routine of Sathya Sai. Before your eyes you can experience divinity exploring its own wonders and relive the invigorating impact great souls like the Buddha, Christ and Shirdi Sai have had on their followers. Here you feel you are in touch with love's reality as you experience the exhilaration of being in the presence of a person who radiates the bliss of the spirit.

The most quoted chronicler of Sai Baba's life is N. Kasturi, a retired professor of history, whose rendering of events is designed to charm the un-inquisitive devotee with mythological references. Since the whole exercise is to strengthen faith, the demands of objectivity (like the sources of his stories) are invariably ignored. Thus, the reader is led to believe that 'Shirdi Baba's tonga' (kept in the Puttaparthi ashram museum), for example, was actually used by the fakir, when in fact the supposition is based on the devotees' assumption that he rode in it in his astral form. Allowance has to be made for Kasturi's middle-class interpretation of a world with whose sufferings he is not directly familiar. It is noticeable in his narrative that, despite being a historian, he prefers to dodge the sociological realities of rural poverty and take refuge behind the smokescreen of ancient quick-fix mythology. No one reading *Sathyam Sivam Sundaram*, his life of Sathya Sai in four parts, would guess that behind all the ancient gloss of penitential pioneers, Puttaparthi lies in the heart of the region gripped by Naxalism, modern India's defiant rural agitation against feudal exploitation by landlords. Kasturi, like all gospel writers, is committed to giving us the good news. Just as Jesus in the Holy Land preached against a turbulent background of Jewish nationalism (the nationalists had hoped he would be a violent Messiah who would urge the overthrow of the occupying Roman army), Sathya Sai grew up amidst similarly volatile nationalist ferment but with the difference that at the age of twenty his motherland became free of its foreign oppressor. Kasturi's biography presupposes a devotional Hindu audience, for there are references to Ram and Krishna and their exploits in the Ramayana and Mahabharata on every page. It is clear that both the young guru and his orthodox biographer were fired by the prospect of the restoration of Hinduism's timeless wisdom. But their idealist hopes of the restoration of

'Rama Rajya' would be tempered with the need to adjust to the reality of a modern democracy.

Sathya Sai Baba was born on 23 November 1926, eight years after Shirdi Baba's death, in a narrow village street lined by low lean-to structures of stone and earth, the kind which can be found in every village of this poorly provided area of southern Andhra. The first great miracle in the story of Sathya Sai Baba is how, from such an economically unprepossessing start and socially inferior order, Sathyanarayan (as he was named) emerged as the embodiment of the spiritual ideal of avatar, the divine come to earth to deliver humanity from its bad karma. The second great miracle is how by the sheer force of inner grace this Raju boy overcame the prejudice that attaches to those whose physical attributes and skin colour do not match orthodoxy's notion of the Aryan ('noble') ideal. The original Sanskrit term for caste, *varna* or 'colouring', betrays the ancient though still current superstition that virtue can be equated with pigmentation. The exception to this lies in the spread of the Sathya Sai movement which appeals to people of all races.

As with the founders of all great religious missions, the soothsayers and old wives have had a field day analyzing the omens and portents that heralded the birth of Sathya Sai and what science cannot verify is easily substituted by creative imagination. The symbolism of reverence needs to be understood, as also the compulsion of religion to embroider—for a good cause—those bare patches on an unfolding tapestry of wonder. As with the coming of Christ and the Buddha, it was necessary for the chroniclers of Sathya Sai's arrival to suitably 'edit' the socio-economic circumstances into which he was born. In

Palestine, no stigma attaches to the craft of carpentry and for Jesus to follow the profession of his (theologically modified surrogate) father only serves to increase the wonder that attended on the manger in a Bethlehem inn. The humble birth of Christ has added enormously to his stature as the compassionate friend of the downtrodden but this perception cuts little ice in the Indian tradition where kingship (as with Rama, Krishna and the Buddha) is viewed as the appropriate level at which the divine should enter human affairs. Even amongst the Jews, the sight of Christ riding a common donkey was an affront to the notion of the Messiah whose proper mount would be a war horse.

Sathyanarayan's grandfather Kondama Raju was renowned for his piety. He is known to have taken his elder son, Pedda Venkappa, on a pilgrimage to Srisailam, the site of one of Hinduism's twelve *jyotir linga* shrines. Shiva is worshipped here as Mallikarjuna, probably a corruption of the name of the Buddhist teacher Nagarjuna who was born in the region. The shrine, originally a Buddhist centre, had been taken over first by brahmins and later, in the medieval period, by unorthodox Lingayats, after which it became famous as the abode of the poet-saint Akka Mahadevi.

Kondama Raju had relatives in these wilder parts of Andhra where dacoity was and still is common. He persuaded one of his distant relatives to settle near Puttaparthi and, as part of the agreement, the relative's daughter, Easwaramma, was betrothed to Pedda Venkappa Raju. A photograph of Pedda Venkappa and Easwaramma taken much later, when they accompanied their illustrious son to Rishikesh on a pilgrimage in 1961, shows a typical village couple—small-boned and accustomed to toil, altogether of unremarkable appearance in their homespun clothes. They look awkward before the camera and seem overwhelmed by the attention paid to them as Sai Baba's parents.

The attempts to upgrade the humble and deprived beginnings of Sathya Sai Baba have been thwarted by the sheer weight of evidence on the ground. Anyone can visit Puttaparthi and check on the family status of this modern man of miracles. Unlike many famous godmen who cover the tracks of their modest beginnings, Sai Baba continues to live in the village of his birth along with his family and relatives. And the facts of his life are often ludicrously at variance with those put out by chroniclers eager to distance divinity from the embarrassment of poverty and secure Sathya Sai safely in the orthodox pantheon.

Parents in India are traditionally accorded reverence and, until the birth of their child prodigy, neither Pedda Venkappa nor Easwaramma were known in the village for anything other than the attributes shared by their neighbours—the piety of the womenfolk offsetting the world-affirming habits of their men. Of course, later stories have appeared and been inserted by the chroniclers (without any attempt to authenticate them) to suggest extraordinary parental dreams and visions, but which mother does not dream that her child should be great and good?

Photographs of Sai Baba show that from an early age he proved a willing and natural subject for the photographer. Just as his father and grandfather before him had rejoiced in playing the role of religious heroes in Telugu folk theatre (Sathya Sai's family was renowned for the dramatization of religious epics in Telugu), Sathyanarayan Raju flourished in a whole array of related fields—acting, directing and script writing. The child inherited his father's love of music and Telugu drama, heavily influenced by the themes of the local folk religion spliced on to the greater vehicle of the Hindu epics. Although he would later forbid his disciples to indulge in polemics, as a boy he delighted in writing ribald verse exposing the hypocrisy of the village moneylender.

In a photo taken on Kondama Raju's hundredth birthday, Sathya Sai (as he had by then chosen to call himself) wears the coloured silk robe and sports the halo hairstyle that would become his identifying marks in public. The old man, clearly full of years, is characterized by the family feature of large ears with elongated lobes. (According to the soothsayers this is a sure sign of an enlightened person!) What is striking is the casual pose of the grandson leaning familiarly on his grandfather's shoulder as if it were that of a favoured disciple. Normally, Indian custom is unforgiving of any disrespect shown towards seniority, yet here is a teenager confidently staring into the camera, casually announcing that his awareness of the agelessness of his own soul puts the age of his grandfather's physical body into the shade.

It is this inner grace and outer poise demonstrated continuously by Sathya Sai from his early years that has led generations of devotees to conclude that this person, irrespective of his humble village origins, exemplifies an awesome, unchanging power. The photograph with Kondama Raju is not just an example of the counterpoint of agile youth to the decrepitude of age. It is evidence of a glowing inner fire in the young man alongside its near extinction in the all too mortal frame of the old. Undoubtedly, this majestic inner glow helped Sathyanarayan persuade first the village boys and then the adults to take his mission of compassionate regard for all life forms seriously. Other village boys obviously jeered at the young do-gooder and bullied him to try and bring his idealism down to their rough, earthly level. He, however, possessed the inner strength of a born leader with a charisma so strong it became a source of irritation to his father who could not fathom the reason for his son's outgoing nature.

Unlike the father who was awkward and fearful when confronted with authority, the son was supremely confident and faced adults with a calmness that suggested not only an old soul but a very remarkable one. At school he was a model student and picked up things so fast he would have been deemed precocious were it not for the fact that his interests lay not in formal learning but in directly apprehending the nature of the soul. The last thing his cash-strapped father, living in a small space with a large joint family wanted, was a dreamy non-productive son. Pedda Venkappa's family had to sacrifice a lot to educate their elder son Seshama Raju who, in the family tradition, proved himself a bright student of Telugu and won the title of 'vidvan' to become an accomplished teacher of the language. He brought much-needed money to the family whereas Sathyanarayan's even brighter talents appeared to be dissipating in his concern to help others instead of furthering his own schooling. There is nothing more exasperating for poor parents than to have a son with generous instincts and the conviction that the Almighty will provide.

There was a running battle between the boy's charitable nature and the father's insistence that he buckle down to a normal schooling. The mother was more understanding but grieved that this unusually tender son of hers attracted so much unwanted attention for his distinctly odd behaviour. From an early age he had the disconcerting habit of materializing sweets, fruits and small objects like pens for his school-going friends. When asked where he got these objects, he said they were presents from the resident goddess of the village. (The Sai Parampara favours the materialization of devotional mementos, calling them the 'visiting cards' from the deathless realm where our souls have their true home. The objective is to nudge doubters towards the awareness that, at its most basic level, religion is not about whether a man believes in God but whether he has experienced that he is more than his body.) Later, a tamarind tree on a hillock would provide his early devotees with a selection of different fruits. This 'kalpavriksha' (wish-fulfilling tree) is one of the few Islamic connections in Puttaparthi since the tamarind is revered by Muslims but not considered sacred by Hindus. Particularly intriguing was the boy's habit of waving his hand palm-down in a series of small vigorous circles from which, as though drawn from a vortex, a fine, almost white ash would appear between the thumb and the forefinger. To the casual bystander it could resemble the sleight of hand of a professional magician, except for the feeling of beatitude conjured up by the young swami (as he would soon be called). Whereas the magician uses manual dexterity and the sluggishness of human reactions to deceive, the skill that Sathyanarayan displayed was of the soul. He had to invest psychic energy to produce the

vibhuti; it was not just a physical trick. Before the magic
of Sathya Sai, both mind and soul are overlaid with a
sense of wonder. The feeling is totally different, of
profundity rather than deceit.

What is the significance of this substance and why do
those who receive it treasure it? It would appear that
vibhuti was the first tangible evidence of the link between
Shirdi Sai and Sathya Sai. For more than half a century
the Shirdi fakir had tended his dhuni, a sacred flame in
his mosque. It is the custom among certain sects of
unorthodox holy men (as well as the duty of the Parsi
priesthood) to keep a fire going as a symbol of life's
underlying energy, an echo of the sun's undying inspiration
behind all mortal concerns, a means to lead our gaze
deeper to the spiritual realm where the 'home fire' of the
soul burns. The production or materialization of this
sacred ash has the power to arouse wonder in the
ordinary person whose awareness of the boundless forces
concealed in his soul is dimmed by the deadening round
of daily routine. We all know at some time in our lives
that we are more than the body. Sathya Sai's *chamatkar*
(display of miraculous powers) rekindles this awareness
by demonstrating the reality of the psychic realm through
which physical manifestation can be reconnected to its
spiritual source.

Sathyanarayan's strange concerns and even stranger
behaviour forced his father to conclude he was possessed.
Unaware of the real power at work and lacking the
understanding to recognize true religion, Pedda Venkappa
took the boy to a witch doctor to be exorcized of his
demons. This consisted of the crudest of all religious
rites. The boy was humiliated and traumatized by being

placed in a pit of liquid manure up to his neck, then tortured, with his head scored and painful potions rubbed on it, as the quack tantric screamed and ranted to impress the faithless family. Apart from the likelihood of his hearing having been permanently impaired, the unruffled Sathyanarayan emerged from the ordeal unrepentant.

His out-of-the-ordinary behaviour and largesse continued and still the woodenness of his father's perceptions refused to yield. The father's impotence before Sathyanarayan's increasing fame in the locality, and his adoption of what seemed to be spiritual airs beyond the station of a Raju, made a confrontation inevitable. Furious at being made to purify himself before entering the presence of his upstart son, the father made to strike him with a lathi—the last argument of peasants. The boy's followers were now too many and too zealous to allow any injury to their young teacher and the disarmed parent could only splutter forth a bewildered, 'Who *are* you?'

A compromise was reached between the spiritually precocious son and his bewildered family. He would return from neighbouring Uravakonda (where he had been lodged with his elder brother) to Puttaparthi but on his terms: he would live near but not with his parents and be free to follow his religious mission. Though his parents may not have had the same level of understanding as their son, they displayed a remarkable inner poise when confronted by this baffling conundrum. It would have been easy for both the sides to break off the relationship in a huff. Indian tradition anyway encourages those who feel the urge to discover God to snap all ties, not just with their immediate relatives but with familiar society. The brick-red robe worn by the Hindu sanyasi is held to represent the colour of the leaping flames of his funeral pyre, signifying that the seeker after God is now dead to all worldly concerns.

Sathyanarayan's family possessed the wisdom to welcome their estranged son as a guest in Puttaparthi to show that though they did not understand his spiritual status, they intuited its genius and were ready to risk honouring it in public. It was a big gamble on their part, for the Indian countryside is no stranger to fake gurus and those inflated by their ability to produce that very *siddhi* (power) of materialization which their son possessed.

It is to Sathyanarayan's credit that he too had implicit trust in his family's word that they would not interfere in his calling. He was still a teenager and in need of parental care. It could have been an explosive situation. Only those unfamiliar with the exacting demands the Hindu joint family places on its dependents to submit themselves entirely to the dictates of their elders will fail to see how revolutionary this treaty between the Rajus was. It offended local religious custom and stood all societal norms on its head. Yet it happened and was effected peacefully—an extraordinary comment on the inner quality this family possessed, and the best evidence of where Sai Baba's innate grace sprang from.

We do not need the mythological intervention of ancient rishis predicting great things for the settlements of Shirdi and Puttaparthi, nor do we require self-playing instruments twanging to announce the birth of a saviour. The simple miracle of an honest farmer and his wife performing their dharma for the well-being of their child prodigy against their better instincts is the best evidence of a divine source at work. Their spiritual status may seem to some to have been exaggerated by the building of temples over their remains, but the fact remains that Venkappa Raju and Easwaramma embodied a rare generosity. They took back a son and provided him both freedom and love, the very things it was Sathya Sai's mission to encourage in his followers.

*

The first mention of the name Shirdi Sai appears in Sathya Sai's life when Sathyanarayan, as a boy, formed his friends into a group of bhajan singers based on the Pandharpur varkari tradition and reference was made to Shirdi in the hymns they sang. While recording this fact, Kasturi puts the question, 'How did this little boy get inspired by that Muslim (?) Fakir?' By inserting the question mark after the word Muslim, he betrays the same orthodox instinct to Hinduize the saint that characterizes the original Shirdi devotees. This is revealing of how even highly educated seekers close to the guru are either reluctant or incapable of letting go of religious labels. Kasturi started out as a sceptic and, as is often the case with a convert, became the most attached of believers. Interestingly, in the edition of the biography published in America (where the author could expect a more critical audience), the query after 'Muslim' was dropped. However, it includes the claim—by implication—that Shirdi Sai wore an 'orange' robe, though it is well attested by his Hindu contemporaries that Shirdi Sai's kafni was uncoloured. In another potentially misleading detail, Kasturi relates how Shirdi Baba established himself in a ruined temple, a slip of the pen that may betray more wishful thinking.

In 1940, at the age of fourteen, Sathyanarayan announced that he did not belong to the Raju clan and was Shirdi Sai returned to earth. 'I am Sai Baba,' the boy said in Uravakonda. At first sight, the contrast between the untidy and irascible figure of the Shirdi fakir and the poor but immaculately clad and well-behaved boy from Puttaparthi seems to preclude any similarity of purpose or outlook. No one in Puttaparthi had heard of the Shirdi fakir, but a minor official in neighbouring Penukonda was discovered to be a devotee and emissaries were sent from Sathyanarayan's family to see if this person could recognize any authenticity in the boy's claims to be a reincarnation. The devotee disappointed them by finding no resemblance whatsoever. Helpfully, he suggested that the boy might be put in a lunatic asylum! However, because of its hoary acceptance of the doctrine of reincarnation, Sathya Sai's claims were of a nature that village India could, after the initial impact, learn to digest.

In those days, Puttaparthi was a dirty, scruffy backwater where poor people had no choice but to litter their surroundings. In spite of this poverty and air of hopelessness, the seed of the spirit found fertile ground here, as if to demonstrate that no challenge is too great for the creative power of life. 'You are born to learn how not to be born again' was the thrust of Sai Baba's message, modifying the traditional Indian view that moksha (release) is the aim of religion. (Release implies rejection of bondage while learning about the nature of the soul leads to fulfilment.) Puttaparthi's headman was a brahmin and his wife Karnam Subbamma was the first to recognize and encourage Sathyanarayan's spiritual gifts. It was Subbamma who provided land for a hut for the returning schoolboy turned swami, where he launched his mission. Later Sathya Sai moved to a long shed with a tin roof (that came to be known as the Old Temple) at the end of the lane where he was born. Today, the site is marked by his father's memorial. The site for the development of the ambitious Prasanthi Nilayam ashram was inaugurated on Baba's birthday in 1950. The initial work was done both by the guru and the volunteers' personal labour. When the problem of dragging girders over the rough interior terrain proved impossible to resolve, Sathya Sai intervened to give engineering advice and even sat with a crane driver to keep up the momentum of the work. This close involvement with every detail of the emerging campus matched Sai Baba's concern for the development of Puttaparthi village, where his family still resides and are counted amongst his closest devotees.

7

Waxing Strong in Spirit

Even in the early days, what was remarkable about the young guru of Puttaparthi was his unshakable and unfathomable self-assurance. Unlike a precocious entrepreneur who takes a huge risk in an investment that may or may not pay off, the youthful Sathya Sai seemed to know exactly what he was about, much like other prodigies of nature gifted with awesome talents. At no point in Sathya Sai's career can the slightest faltering of vision or dragging of step be detected. From poor and primitive beginnings his has been a triumphant march which culminated, with an almost casual panache, in the seemingly unattainable goal of acceptance as a world teacher.

The miraculous or, certainly, the super-normal nature of Sai is reflected in the calm and purposeful unfolding of the young Sathya Sai's agenda for the expansion of his village's welfare. A notable trait of the young Master was that he brooked no interference with the unfolding of his master plan. Where did this callow youth's confidence come from? He would listen to advice but more, it seemed, out of courtesy then because he needed it. Old disciples with a lifetime of senior administrative experience soon learned that the only advice that mattered was confirmation of Sathya Sai's own decision. Having served big figures in the government, it came as a shock for these advisors to find a young man who not only knew his own mind but understood the minds of those who sought to advise him.

It was as though Sathya Sai visualized the vast Prasanthi Nilayam ashram campus and his own role in it from the beginning, not necessarily from the omniscience that is associated with the role of avatar but from an assured faith in his calling. Convinced that he was the chosen vehicle of Shirdi Baba's divine powers, he surrendered his personality to the inflow of spirit, knowing that it could only lead to a compassionate outcome. In addition to being the catalyst for Puttaparthi's dramatic outer development, he was the inner witness who inspired its spiritual direction. Neither of these roles drained his energy, rather they recharged it. It was as if he knew that both he and his mission were sent forth by the divine, and his work was only to reaffirm the hand of the spirit. The growth of Baba's 'Abode of Well-Being' would happen because it was *graced* to happen. This measureless well of faith which the young guru drew on to shape his early mission helps explain why he always seemed impervious to the worry and agitation that seems to plague most ashrams trying to balance their programmes and budgets. Gurdjieff's institute was forever in financial straits and eventually collapsed from failure to pay the rent. Gurdjieff however was unfazed by the crash. Like Sathya Sai, he understood the essential benevolence of the life force and knew that the inner teaching can never be dependent on outer structures.

. Sathya Sai seems indifferent to the inner teaching. In some mysterious way he is the embodiment of the teaching itself. He has no guru because he needs none. He was born not to teach but to be. In his being is the teaching. This explains why intellectuals have been prone to view the philosophy of the Sai Parampara as rather amorphous, lacking a pronounced stance and displaying little regard for scholastic niceties. But why do we need to read a dead text when the living author stands before us? One more prophet announcing one more religion is not Sathya Sai's spiritual brief. By reaffirming the compassionate concerns of Shirdi Baba, the Puttaparthi master preaches the essential oneness of all religions. Though the Sathya Sai mission appeared to be heading towards orthodoxy in the early days, this was a necessary tactic to include the weight of respectable opinion. In reality, Sai himself isn't partial to any particular religious line but encourages us to recognize what is common to them all. We have to celebrate the joy of the spirit, unconcerned by the different shapes and brands of the bottles in which the elixir is contained.

This is why there are so few outer trappings of religion at Puttaparthi: no formal initiation, no conversion, no sacred text, no creed, no ritual, no indoctrination, no priesthood, no temple, no donation box. The aim is to facilitate the merging of the soul with its creator. The great stimulus is the presence of Sai Baba himself whose cosmic love treads the Deccan soil, exuding unearthly grace. There is no Sai religion, only Sai love. The purpose of the new campus, envisioned all along by the boy saint, is to shake us out of our small denominational certainties so that we can experience the essential spirit that informs all the world's religions. For this reason, at the heart of the campus is the Sarva Dharma Stupa, built by the sweat and toil of the ashram inmates who lined up like a chain gang to pass the building material, symbolizing how the congregation had taken on the responsibility of a kind of self-ordained priesthood. Many volunteers feel their flow of devotion to Sai Baba elevates them to the level of an agent of the divine. The pillar with its flowering lotus of respect for all religions rises as a symbol of the indivisibility of love.

Many visitors to the ashram pooh-pooh such idealistic signposts and point to the frustrations, bitterness and personal animosities that characterize relations among the devotees. They overlook the possibility that these imperfections may be the best proof of mental and spiritual transformation. An ashram without friction is simply not doing its job to change people. Such a process is painful and sparks will fly. As with all relationships based on intense love, envy is a close neighbour who sits alongside, especially when it appears that the master is playing favourites. Each devotee has his own level of awareness. Only those who are not content to be passive witnesses to their shortcomings will strive to achieve a better understanding of why their behaviour falls short of the ideal. The childhood conditioning of caste and creed is not easy to overthrow and the devotees gather here to give it a try. That they fail is often true, but before them stands the example of the master who, having risen above the clamour of the world, dwells in the steady glow of the spirit.

What Sathya Sai has accomplished for his village he aims to achieve for the subcontinent. Conventional religion, as it is practised, has failed miserably in many respects and hence his call to rediscover love and nurture compassionate regard for the whole of humanity.

*

Unlike the Buddha and Christ who reached maturity before setting out on their mission, Sathya Sai began teaching at the tender age of fourteen. India is well acquainted with the phenomenon of the *bal brahmachari*, the boy saint whose mission starts with a bang but loses steam when the novelty of youthful dedication wears off. Few saints have had such a long and stable mission as Sathya Sai whose popularity graph continues to soar. The lifestyle of the saint has hardly varied in sixty years of practice. Any desire for physical comfort has been reduced to a minimum and Baba's time is devoted entirely to the welfare of others. In this Puttaparthi version of holy communion it appears that the master and the disciples benefit from one another's company, the teacher responding to the love offered and the disciple gaining charge for his soul's battery. This is no idle analogy. Many devotees experience that charge as a physical reality. Like the woman who touched the hem of Christ's garment and felt instantly healed, many arrivals at Puttaparthi have felt rejuvenated. Sai Baba's electrifying presence is the secret behind all these years of increasing adulation and it accounts for the exponential growth of his following. Physical contact with this person whose own battery never seems to deplete is a tonic. Just a momentary glimpse of Sathya Sai's aura thrills the devotee's soul.

At the outset of his mission, Sathya Sai lived with and shared physical space with his devotees. He moved in 1945 to what would be known as the Old Mandir, an elongated shed with a curtain at one end to provide him some privacy during his interviews with disciples. One-to-one encounters with selected visitors have always been the mark of Sathya Sai's teaching method. During these interviews he invariably 'produces' keepsakes like rings, lockets and ornaments bearing his or Shirdi Sai's portrait. But he may also produce medicine and even provide treatment for those with chronic ailments. The interviews soften up the devotees who are chosen at random. Later, a veranda was tacked on to this structure to accommodate the increasing number of visitors. In the mid-1960s, the overflow was so great that visitors slept on the ground outside, sharing space with snakes and scorpions. Apparently, Puttaparthi's scorpions are famous for their size and sting, and this was a great decider of destinies. Only those prepared to put up with such physical dangers would stay on.

In those days, Baba used to gravitate to the banks of the nearby Chitravati river for evening discourses which would on occasion be punctuated and made memorable by his production of divine images from the sands of the river bed. Despite its seductive name, the Chitravati is strictly a seasonal stream, and after months of desert-like dryness it can suddenly boil over in spate. Invariably, some people saw this as Baba's miraculous intervention, though the hydrology of this district made the pattern of flash floods predictable.

Most of the early visitors were poor people from the surrounding villages but as word of Sai's miraculous nature—to the extent of daily producing vibhuti and other small objects at will—got around, visitors started coming from further afield. Sai Baba's brother was upset when some of these rich visitors took Baba off to Bangalore and Mysore in their cars, worrying that his brother would be corrupted by being pitchforked into the unaccustomed life of the big city. Like his father, the elder son was conventional in outlook and unable to fathom the imperturbability of Sathya Sai's soul. Nothing happened to the boy. Neither was his head turned nor was he impressed by anything other than his host's genuine devotion. Unlike his elders, he knew that devotion had nothing to do with social status, age or wealth. After these trips out of Puttaparthi, the fame of the boy saint spread throughout the south and visits further away in answer to devotees' prayers inevitably followed.

Kasturi has described the most significant turning point in the young guru's career. Sathya Sai, a frequent visitor to Tirupati, charmed Raja Sarvagna Kumar Krishna Yachendra of Venkatagiri, a small state of cultural distinction situated near Kalahasti, not far from Tirupati. The raja was a sincere and orthodox Hindu and so completely enthralled by the presence of Sai Baba that he was not ashamed to declare it in public. When Baba visited the town of Venkatagiri, the raja would roll in the dust in front of the saint's car in dramatic demonstration of the traditional belief that the true king is one who possesses the abilty to recognize true greatness. Inevitably, this exaggerated royal behaviour was reported far and wide and, thanks to the esteem in which he was held by orthodox society, the raja's recognition of Sathya Sai's spiritual status intrigued many Hindus who had only heard rumours about this rustic miracle-worker. The worldly-wise raja understood the stigma attached to the young teacher's caste and shrewdly set about refurbishing Sathya Sai's socio-religious credentials. In 1957, a conference of pundits and savants was convened at Venkatagiri and Sathya Sai was introduced to a critical audience comprising high-powered figures of Hindu orthodoxy. The charm that had won over the raja extended to the gathered saints and they went away amazed at the young guru's poise, apparent scholarship and indisputable authority.

After this, Sai Baba was invited to Rishikesh to meet Swami Shivananda, a pilgrimage that marked his entry into mainstream Hindu culture. Swami Shivananda was a doctor of south Indian descent from Malaysia, generous, kindly and well connected. When I visited his ashram (the year Baba made his second visit) I noted that the heavily-built swami would donate a pile of his own books to every visitor. He had an abundance of energy and good humour and made pilgrims of all faiths warmly welcome in his ashram. Significantly, the swamis who extended the invitation advised Baba to cool his heels in Puttaparthi before venturing north. They knew well the prejudice and jealousy that exist between different schools and ashrams, and they had to convince their own gurus first that this boy saint was a genuine teacher worthy of popular Hindu respect. Up till now rumour had painted him as a magician, a boy who attracted public attention not because of his teaching but because of his psychic powers.

This tour to Rishikesh was followed four years later

by the arduous pilgrimage to Badrinath in the company
of the Governor of Uttar Pradesh. To be part of any
governor's entourage is an accolade of respectability in
the eyes of the public. Only a few years earlier, like Shirdi
Baba, the Puttaparthi saint had to be content with petty
officials at the base of India's pyramid of political
authority.

The Badrinath darshan was marked by the unexpected
materialization of a special Kailash lingam, unexpected
because the temple is dedicated to Vishnu. This incident
is revealing of how little south-Indians are aware of the
historical realities in the north. Kasturi claims that
Shankaracharya had established Jyotirmath (the winter
seat of the deity) 'to counteract Buddhist influences that
threatened to percolate through the Mana Pass', but
Buddhism had barely arrived in Tibet during this period.
Another doubtful claim (made by the priests at Badrinath)
is that the Buddhists had thrown the image of Badrinath
into the river, and Shankaracharya then reinstalled it.
However, the image worshipped at Badri is actually that
of the Buddha, so why should the Buddhists throw it out?
(The Buddha's *padmasana* posture is concealed from
pilgrims by floral offerings.) Kasturi explains the reason
for Baba producing a lingam at a Vaishnav shrine. He
says that Vishnu had 'resorted to a stratagem' to take
possession of what was originally a Shaivite shrine. This
is the same phrase used by historians for the brahminical
takeover of the Buddhist shrine at Srisailem. The taking
over of shrines in India has always been commonplace
but orthodox Hindus prefer to blame this custom on
monotheists.

Between these visits north, Baba travelled through the

delta area of Andhra, receiving a rousing reception wherever he went. His eminence as a teacher was growing and, slowly but surely, he was outgrowing his boyhood reputation of being a mere miracle monger. He consolidated his orthodox base in these first few missionary journeys through Andhra, his poetic talents with Telugu being put to good use for the purpose. In his discourses he had to follow a conventional line in order to be taken seriously, thus echoing Shirdi Baba's dictum that if you want people to hear what you have to say, you first have to tell them what they want to hear. What this translated to in practice was that Baba regaled his audiences with myths from the Puranas. Once he had their attention he would introduce the profounder spiritual insights of the Upanishads. This transition to a deeper level of understanding however would take a whole generation to accomplish.

A visit to Srisailem in 1963 was followed two years later by Baba's darshan of Vitthal, the most egalitarian of Hindu deities at Pandharpur. Many of the bhajans sung at Puttaparthi recapture the mood of rustic devotion unique to Pandharpur. This was followed by a controversial retreat into ritual orthodoxy in Andhra where Sathya Sai presided over an elaborate yagna at which two lakh spoonfuls of ghee were consumed. Modern India is quick to spot the bizarre contrast between a starving peasantry and its religiously narcissistic landlords who waste the fruits of the land on elaborate Vedic rites. However, in this instance, the starving victims were poor brahmins whose livelihood depended on performing rituals. They had all been made redundant, their dharmic duties swept away by modernity. In championing their rights

Sai Baba may have agitated the supporters of the Left but reaped a rich harvest in winning popular Hindu sympathies.

Sai Baba was well aware that a people's war was being fought outside Andhra's rich delta area. But he knew that without the support of the rich landlords he would not be able to extend his mission to the leaner areas of the state. He took a long-term view of the people's struggle against injustice, realizing, like Gurdjieff, that to take sides rigidly would help no one. Gurdjieff had continued his mission during the height of the Bolshevik takeover of Czarist Russia. Aware of the short-term nature of political change, he made sure to remain friendly with both the sides but not get too close to either. If he had taken sides he would have been eliminated. Thanks to his foresight, now that communism has disappeared, his remarkable teachings are still available to the seeker.

By indulging the landlords' religious sentiments, Sathya Sai created a fund of goodwill backed by a promise to underwrite his mission. But the problem of flirting too closely with the reactionary end of society was that Sai Baba sometimes was portrayed as sounding uncomfortably akin to a Hindu zealot. Remarks like 'the rest of the community care only for feeding and breeding' could easily be misconstrued as a criticism of non-Hindus. At the founding of the Indian Academy of Vedic Scholars in 1965, Baba spoke of the Goddess Bhavani giving Shivaji a sword to 'uphold Hinduism'. This subliminal hint of a militant riposte to the sword of Islam went down well with the Hindutva brigade and Sai Baba's mission was invited to join forces with the Vishwa Hindu Parishad, the cheerleader movement of anti-minority activism. Its leaders would become a regular presence on the mandir veranda at Puttaparthi in later years, though this is as far as their influence would penetrate.

In 1967, Baba made an excursion to Jamnagar whose ruling family had become his close followers. Being a much wealthier ex-state than Venkatagiri, it was in a position to provide the regalia that the Sai Parampara has always delighted in. We have already seen Shirdi Baba's love for ceremonial processions because they lent some colour to drab village life. The most popular gift to Puttaparthi must be the magnificent silver *jhula* gifted by the rajmata of Jamnagar. Sai Baba swings on it ritually every year on his birthday, in an elegant affirmation of the Vaishnav tradition of Kathiawad, centred at the pilgrim town of Dwarka. The rajmata of Jamnagar would, in fact, prove such a generous donor in the construction of both Prasanthi and Whitefield that Baba rewarded her with a house near his own at both ashrams.

1968 marked Sathya Sai's one and only journey abroad—to Uganda. The visit was remarkable for the frenetic reception accorded to Baba by the Africans. Amongst the most welcoming was defence chief Idi Amin who danced in front of Baba's car. The Indian business community which had invited Baba were urged to be more sensitive to the host nation's feelings lest envy of the Indians' success turn to hostility. Four years later, Baba's prediction about Uganda came true. The Asians were expelled and their businesses taken over.

On his return to India, Baba drove to Anantapur to acquire the land for the planned ladies' college. This marked the big breakthrough in his educational expansion programme and, together with the hospital he set up at his mother's bidding way back when he started out on his mission, reveals Baba's concern for the physical welfare of the community in general.

That winter, Sai Baba expanded his base by entering the staunch Shaivite country of north Kannada and winning them over to the extent of teaching them hymns to Krishna which they sang in their temples. Though it sounds like a minor regional coup, it was, in fact, a revolutionary stroke, for Sai Baba was able to soften centuries of inflexible spiritual pride. Next was a visit to Goa where he stayed with Governor Nakul Sen and his wife Indu who were followers of the Aurobindo ashram in Pondicherry. Nakul Sen was highly regarded for his administrative acumen. A medical miracle occurred during this stay which was witnessed and verified by Nakul Sen. Baba refused surgery and healed himself of acute appendicitis, apparently by will-power—to confound all professional prognostications. Because of the governor's reputation for integrity, this event received wide media attention.

Baba made further visits to north India in the 1970s, 80s and 90s. He was the ideal guest, proving not only undemanding but generous in every way with his time and energy. People rich and poor, from towns and surrounding villages came round the clock to see him and he gave darshan to them whenever the opportunity arose. Those who had only heard the usual rumours of him being a black magician were impressed by the modesty of his appearance and talk. They were able to see how vested interests and religious rivals deliberately spread these stories to try and confuse the public. To be with

Baba at close quarters is an unforgettable experience, not because of any Godlike awe he arouses, but for the opposite reason—the wonderfully human touch he displays, showing tender concern for all, expressed in the most natural way. The grace of a rare being seems to shine through him and when he stayed for three days in Mussoorie I got the distinct impression (making him different from all the other saints I have met) of an abiding awareness. Normally, we view grace as a portion of the divine but here the fullness of Providence seemed to brim over.

From 1980 onwards, for several years, Baba held a summer course for students at his Whitefield campus in the month of June. Whitefield is a three-hour car journey from Puttaparthi and it was convenient for Baba to retire there when the festival crowds at Puttaparthi became overwhelming. As long as he was in residence in the village, the crowds were loathe to go home. But Whitefield is a much smaller campus and if Baba stayed here too long, there was little chance of a darshan for his main following. Baba, being very alive to the economic needs of simple vendors who make a living out of the crowds drawn to Puttaparthi, arranges his programme so that these daily wage earners do not suffer unduly because of his absence. Those who harp on his penchant to mix with rich industrialists and ex-royals overlook that these devotees have to come to his village to see him on his terms. The reality is that he spends a great deal of his time with his poorer devotees. Diana Baskin records how Baron Albert Rothschild, one of the richest men in America, came to meet Baba but, instead of seeing him, Baba went to meet a party of devotees so poor they had been forced to walk all the way from Nepal. To show his appreciation, Baba invited them to eat with him. Sharing food with the poor is another grace constantly seen at Puttaparthi. During communal meals, Sathya Sai personally serves the visitors and shows no disgust at touching beggars, lepers and society's outcastes. Nor does he hold women impure during their periods.

By the 1990s, Sathya Sai was such an important national figure that his ashram had become a tourist venue for pilgrims and was included in international guidebooks. His presence had become such a draw that it began to have an impact on the national economy. He collects such crowds that his travel had to be restricted due to security concerns. Arrival by air in the capital, for example, would draw huge numbers, exceeding any which gathered to welcome VIPs.

For some years, Baba made annual visits to Kodaikanal. He was concerned that every detail in food, transport and accommodation be perfect. He showed a personal interest in checking these arrangements and was a stickler for protocol. Though scenic to behold, Kodai has a chronic shortage of accommodation and Baba could not linger long since the crowds who gathered for his darshan had nowhere to stay. On these visits by road, Baba's convoy would halt at dozens of villages en route to receive the welcome of local Sai samitis. In return, Baba would bless these small but genuine efforts to practise his message. They were the best evidence of the success of his teaching.

The dawn of the twenty-first century was celebrated with Baba's birthday gift of Chaitanya Jyoti, an exciting architectural creation endowed with cosmic beauty and dedicated to the unity of religions. Significantly, if you peep into the elegant meditation hall, not a soul is visible inside. The crowds are all down the road, before the living temple of Sathya Sai, now (in 2004) a frail, physically diminishing figure but as effulgent as ever, radiating the ineffable grace of the Sai Parampara.

*

Baba's almost casual acquaintance with any religion outside the familiar beat of Hinduism showed during his visit to the former sultanate of Bijapur where he apparently showed little interest in seeing the spectacular Islamic buildings that make this town one the world's richest architectural sites. It was also demonstrated by the fact that though Sathya Sai visited the town of Navsari on several occasions, not a single mention is made by his biographers of the fact that this is the most sacred seat of the Parsi religion. This surprising lack of information about other religious traditions comes out clearly in a conversation Sathya Sai had with John Hislop (an American devotee) regarding the Puttaparthi ashram logo which aims to include the major religions of the world. In fact, it omits Judaism (among others) and since Sai Baba has many followers belonging to the Jewish faith, several of them queried why their symbol, the Star of David, had been left out. According to Hislop, Baba was genuinely surprised at the complaint and asked if Jews were 'substantially' aggrieved at having the Christian cross stand in for their religion! In view of the horrific fallout of the anti-Semitism almost inbuilt into Christendom, it seems extraordinary that anyone, let alone Sathya Sai, could be so unaware of the deep divisions that have racked Europe for centuries. Or is Baba's concern to subtly heal a rift between faiths that share (in part) a common scripture? Neither Sikh nor Jain symbols are shown on the ashram logo but, because of the absence of any cultural rift, the followers of these faiths accept the *aum* symbol.

However, a noticeable change would come over Baba's outlook after exposure to foreign delegates at the first World Conference of Sai Baba Organizations in Bombay in 1968. Up until then he had been influenced by Hindu organizations who hoped to harness his popularity to spread their own agenda. Sathya Sai refused to get involved with these politico-religious movements although he might have shared their cultural concerns. Thus, the Ram Janmabhumi agitation in Ayodhya which culminated in the destruction of the Babri Masjid by Hindu fanatics found little favour with Sai Baba. He categorically stated as early as 1961 that limiting Rama to Ayodhya was to deny his full glory. This suggests Sai Baba was conscious of the way the name of Rama was being cynically utilized for political gain and made sure, by distancing himself from chauvinist organizations of any persuasion, that similar use would not be made of his own name.

8

God in Three Persons

The word 'Sai' is akin to the Biblical 'Lord', as is the expression 'Swami' which is how most devotees refer to Sathya Sai. Whereas Swami denotes 'master of oneself', Sai connotes a more avuncular image. Thus the Sai Parampara is softer in its perception of divinity and differs from the Semitic view of God as a despotic controller of human destiny. The term 'Sai' can also be used as an endearment between wife and husband and is suffused as much with human affection as spiritual regard. So too is the word 'Bhagavan' which conveys exactly the blend of awe and familiarity that characterizes the Bhakti approach to divinity.

The informal approach to religion, the lack of dogma and absence of rituals that characterize the Sai Parampara's understanding of spirituality are also visible in its insistence on a normal life which seeks to steer clear of religion's two extreme besetting sins—greed for wealth and its opposite, the despising of wealth as ungodly. Both Shirdi and Sathya Sai have encouraged engagement with the world and opposed the theatrics of penance and renunciation. They share the essayist Addison's dignified assessment of true belief: 'Those who make religion to consist in contempt of this world and its enjoyments are under a very fatal and dangerous mistake. As life is the gift of heaven, it is religion to enjoy it. He, therefore, who can be happy in himself, and who contributes all in his power toward the happiness of others, answers most effectually the ends of his creation, is an honour to his nature, and a pattern to mankind.' Neither Shirdi's fakir robes nor Sathya Sai's orange gown signifies any actual distancing of the sacred from the common. The spirit is not an affair solely for priests and holy men to delve into but the common property of any human soul who lays claim to it. Real religion boils down to compassion for creation, derived from our feeling of oneness with it. The reformist spirit of the Shirdi and Sathya Sai recognizes that the world's problems can be solved not by people converting to other faiths but by the followers of any given religion practising more earnestly the precepts of their own faith. We must honour our religion by demonstrating a love so infectious it will convert all doubters to our cause. The Deccan saints did found a new religion but one within the heart, beyond all labels. Furthermore, it is not a joyless compromise with a flawed, illusory or sinful world as put out by most religions. Shirdi and Sathya Sai teach a refreshing gospel that celebrates creation and finds in life nothing so disgusting as cannot be remedied by an infusion of love. Sathya Sai actively encourages his devotees to marry and is happy to arrange their marriages for them. He will also bless mass marriages of couples since this saves them the expenses that villagers, in the name of religion, ruinously invest in. From feeding a baby its first mouthful of rice to overseeing the rites of cremation, Sathya Sai shows a motherly concern for all.

Though absorbed in the realm of the spirit, this strange young teacher has always kept one foot in the world, his status always defying easy categorization. The problem is that the usual rules do not seem to apply to him. Rather, even more inexplicably, he appears to be the rule maker. Although seemingly religious in his behaviour, he wears no signs whatsoever of any caste or religious affiliation: no tilak painted on the forehead, no talisman on the wrist, no beads round his neck, no wearing of any sacred thread, no worship of any god nor genuflection to any guru.

To the student of religion his presence is a conundrum, for no such figure since the days of Christ has so elegantly walked the earth. After thirty years of viewing this unvarying statement of grace, I have to admit that Sathya Sai's spiritual certainty has not wavered one bit. He needs none of the trappings of religion it seems because he carries within himself the light of which these are all a reflection. If he wears an orange robe, it is not because he has renounced the world but because it conveniently enables him to stand out in public and allows more people to spot him during mass darshan. Neither the colour (which can vary according to season) nor the texture of the material (which can raise the eyebrows of the orthodox) has any religious significance whatsoever. It is a detail, unimportant in relation to what the wearer has come to teach. At the same time, the detail is symbolic. The robe is always fresh and well laundered, covering the entire body to indicate that the mystery this man embodies does not yield to any physical explanation.

Strangely, though aloof to the outer signs of religion, he understands every detail of Hindu ritual and custom. If he had been a practising Muslim in a former life, how is this possible? If he had been born a Hindu and brought up as a Muslim, that would imply his wisdom dates from an even earlier incarnation. (When Shirdi Baba had to give evidence in a case of theft, he answered the question of how old he was by replying 'lakhs of years'.) The short answer seems to be that Sathya Sai (like Shirdi Baba before him) is altogether unique. Whether you attribute that uniqueness to the play of the divine or to the odd conjunction of natural forces, the fact is, this person is like no other in his resolve. Men and women weep openly at the beauty revealed before them. When his energy is discharged, it seems immediately replaced in a baffling denial of all known physical laws. Perhaps the clue lies in our poor understanding of the capacity of the human soul.

Religion is given its due at Puttaparthi but has no relevance to the state Sai Baba has attained. Its language points the way to the devotee and, since the way is difficult, such signposts are helpful. Only the simple will mistake the name of the destination for the destination itself. Those seeking to find the divine within still need the crutch of religion though, significantly, the Sai Parampara insists that the baggage of caste has to be left at the gate. Shirdi and Puttaparthi must be amongst the few places in the whole of India where no overt reference to caste is made. Dr R.T. Kakade recounts in *Shirdi to Puttaparthi* (1985), which he co-authored with

Dr A. Veerbhadra Rao, how the absence of caste discrimination had attracted him to Shirdi Baba.

In showing even regard for different beliefs, Sathya Sai on the one hand encourages traditional respect to be shown to the brahmins who perform public ceremonies at his ashram. On the other hand he shows personal interest in the welfare of Puttaparthi's Muslims whose mosque he helped to enlarge.

Reading about the life and teachings of Shirdi Sai, it is noticeable how most of the devotees in his lifetime were Hindus forced to overcome their inherited prejudice against a Muslim saint. That they did so is a remarkable testimony not just to the saint's outer aura but to their own inner strength. Triumphing over cultural conditioning and serious mental reservations, true religion was honoured by these trusting disciples. Recognizing the valour of these bhaktas who, against all norms, chose to worship a fakir in a mosque, Shirdi Sai in turn went against the feelings of his fellow Muslims in allowing his Hindu bhaktas to display apparently heretical behaviour. Both master and disciple displayed the bravery that love calls forth and their differing cultural backgrounds could meet, not just in a tumbledown mosque, but in the timeless realm of the Compassionate and Merciful. The orthodox of both faiths, by clinging to their cold assessment of rules, miss out on experiencing the very love which is the essence of the religion they imagine they are championing.

*

Over the last three decades I have made around a dozen visits to Puttaparthi (not as a practising devotee but as a pilgrim to the shrine of love) and have been to Whitefield and Shirdi two times each. My first visit in the late 1970s followed Baba's two visits to Delhi during which he had found time to dine at Rani-ma's house. As I was a new arrival and still conditioned by my training at Mirtola to be very cautious about accepting publicly announced claims to divinity, I was content to watch and reserve judgement. I had to recognize the wonderful influence Sai Baba had on Rani-ma's spirit but found the organization, at least in Delhi, more enthusiastic than inspiring. The main feature was bhajan singing for which I have neither taste nor talent, but more beautiful was the way Rani-ma performed her daily *abhishek* (puja) of a lingam Sai Baba had materialized for her. This she observed no matter what. I was intrigued by the sheen on this lingam; this small but solid object of mixed metals seemed to have a life of its own. I had some experience of worshipping the shalagram in Mirtola but that seemed as distant as its deep-sea origins compared to the vibrant touch of the lingam.

When I arrived in Puttaparthi I was shown to a large shed that accommodated parties of new arrivals like myself and we were all provided a bamboo mat and floor space on which to spread our belongings. The facilities were basic and communal which meant you had to queue up for a tap. This involved a trip to the tiny bazaar to buy an aluminium mug (plastic was still a novelty then).

If Baba was the proverbial welcoming angel, the devotees who ran the ashram offices were something else and could be quite blunt in their attitude to newcomers. I made the mistake of taking the side of a girl who had come all the way from London on a limited schedule and wanted a front seat for darshan. At first I did not take the advice the office gave to the girl graciously but soon came to realize they had no choice in view of the surging demand for such privileges. They had to sound fatalistic and say it was her destiny that would decide. (I also had to admit that had she not been so pretty I would not have troubled my head about her destiny.) Hence, for me, Baba's words had an immediate salutary effect: 'I dislike purposeless conversation between men and women. External beauty and charm are ephemeral. The real beauty is self-control. You are the occupant of the body, not the body.'

Life for the ashram residents was a most tense and exhausting affair and I would learn to account for the rudeness that shocked me on the first occasion. No one had specific jobs, all were volunteers. By putting the onus for running the ashram on his disciples, Baba was forcing them to take responsibility. They had no fixed hours of work, which meant that they were theoretically on duty all the time. Small wonder that their tempers flared when confronted by visitors who viewed the ashram as a kind of spiritual tourist resort.

The unique thing about the ashram is its air of self-discipline that declares itself in the extraordinary quality of silence. This is not enforced but arises from an appreciation that sound is too sacred to be wasted on trivial exchanges. The white cotton uniform also encourages a oneness with the environment though, at the time, I equated it with the negative neta syndrome in Indian politics of scoundrels wearing handloom to appear patriotic. The strangest effect of switching from city clothes to ashram gear is the feeling that one has donned a new and more meaningful identity. It is almost as if one is moving from life to real life.

Compared to Puttaparthi, Shirdi would turn out to be more rustic, and while the devotion was just as intense, the organization—since it was managed by a government-appointed committee—inevitably lent a more mechanical air to the proceedings. In spite of this handicap, the arati to the saint's marble image was done with rapturous devotion. The sheer press of devotees eager for prasad put the pujaris under pressure and a shawl that was offered was barely draped over the shoulders of the saint before being whipped off for the next. To the merely curious, such devotion resembles an assembly line and, for those who expect at least an aesthetic climax to a longed-for darshan, there was nominal disappointment. In spite of all the apparent differences and the gap in time, I found I could at least relate to the same compassionate mood that flowed through both Shirdi and Puttaparthi. Certainly, the shopkeepers who sold trinkets, photographs and vibhuti of the two saints seemed exactly the same at both places, mixing devotion with business and bringing happiness both to their customers and themselves.

*

It seems strange that while Shirdi Baba was identified with a whole list of saints (including Akkalkot Swami, Akunbaba, Gholapguruji, Maulisahib, Ramdas Swami and Saptashringi Devi, not to mention being equated with Ganesh, Rama, Shiva and even Jain Tirthankars), some modern Shirdi devotees strongly object to the idea of Sathya Sai or anyone else as a spiritual successor. It is amusing to note that a few otherwise intelligent devotees scrupulously ignore any reference to Puttaparthi, pretending that Sathya Sai Baba, the greatest religious phenomenon of the age, does not exist! Despite this distancing, the evidence seems to favour some common spiritual tie. The fact that Sathya Sai has preferred to promote the Puttaparthi ashram without any physical reference to Shirdi signifies to many that it is not in the hallowed pilgrim sites of the past that the seeker must look for divinity but where the spirit manifests here and now.

Both saints may have been very different in habit and temperament, yet the psychic and spiritual similarities appear to far outweigh the physical differences. To begin with, both teachers enjoy the rare status of being considered 'unique' in spiritual worth. At the same time, both are the targets of notorious abuse and are violently derided for 'corrupting religion and morality'. Among other things, each has at one time or the other been called a false prophet, an enemy of religion, a sorcerer, a conjuror, a seducer, a pederast, a racketeer, a gold smuggler, an anti-poor obscurantist and a Satanic force.

The reality is something else. Both saints have been known to be delightfully unorthodox in their tastes. Shirdi Baba, after he became famous, would go to perform his ablutions in processional order, perhaps to shock the conventional idea of the reach of holiness. Sathya Sai, attuned to the common man's likes, has built a cricket stadium in Puttaparthi. Shirdi Sai was reputed to be an accomplished healer with deep medical knowledge like Sathya Sai today (who even performs surgical operations).

Shirdi Sai loved music, dance and ceremony, was a skilled cook, gardener (and carrier of water!); favoured a normal householder's life; recommended active engagement with the world; taught surrender to the power of love; was capable of radiating a warmth that captivated; was concerned for his disciples' welfare and provided generously for their needs; had a rich sense of peasant humour; showed no interest in starting any new religion; was indifferent to the performance of any public religious observance such as puja or namaz; opposed asceticism and the display of penitential exercises; accepted the validity of all recognized scriptures and found value in scriptural exegesis; received worship offered to him, not personally but as forms of the divine; was recognized as a form of Dattatreya and accepted the identification; displayed compassion to the poor, downtrodden and society's outcastes; remained untouched by consciousness of caste; taught the oneness of all religions; encouraged the strengthening of the faith into which one was born and opposed conversion of convenience; used sacred ash as a sign of his grace; used psychic phenomena to interact with his disciples; loved nature and animals and inculcated compassionate regard for all lowly forms of life; predicted the expansion of his mission; shared the ability to materialize objects and apparently affect the elements to a limited extent; practised the siddhi of departing the body for up to several days at a time, leaving devotees to conclude he was clinically dead; took the precaution of advising his attendants beforehand of the likely fallout of these withdrawal exercises to make sure no one was allowed to interfere with his body while he was absent; declared that his sometimes serious illnesses had been voluntarily contracted in order to save a favoured disciple from likely death; opposed to the expression of strong opinions in religious matters and refused to engage in debates even to defend his own teaching—and in all of these aspects, he was exactly like Sathya Sai is today.

The unstated theology of the Sai Baba faith is that the divine—the goal, the life force, call it what you will—is the experience of love, the ultimate grace that descends upon the human heart. Enlightenment is nothing but the soul falling in love with its source. Love being larger than ourselves, we are overwhelmed and disoriented by its breathless ineffability. In the throes of unexpected bliss, the ego and mind are temporarily subdued and the soul briefly united with the object of its adoration. The spontaneous igniting of love is the opposite of formal religious worship where the mood of fervency is sought to be built up with the aid of music and ceremony. Love is akin to possessing the kingdom of heaven. It gives us wings and cosmic understanding. We cease from our quest to find God because in love we have found where that mystery dwells.

The Sai Parampara, following the insights of Kabir and concerned with the unsophisticated soul of the masses, urges the devotee to melt in ecstasy before the beloved. This is essentially what Gurdjieff recommended to his much more select following. Until we can surrender to a force higher than our individual ego, the inner teaching will remain an intellectual exercise. 'I can peel [your] potato,' said Gurdjieff, 'but only you can take out the "eyes".' Like Shirdi Sai before him, Sathya Sai promises to grant his disciples everything their hearts want, conditional on surrendering their destiny to the guru. A constant refrain running through the lives of both saints is the question asked by the teacher: 'What do you really want?' When the reply is, 'I only want to be part of you,' the disciple is accepted, though there is no formal acknowledgement. The Sai relationship is an inner bond based on love. Our search for its substitute in power, sex, money and fame occupies most of our energies unless we have the grace to stumble on a compassionate teacher who opens our eyes to the real goal within.

The teacher is the catalyst. We do not surrender ourselves to his dictates as much as consciously decide to suppress our ego to our higher instincts. To touch the feet of a guru really signifies the offering of the intellect to the greater wisdom of the heart. For those brought up to value the brain as the greatest of God-given faculties, it is hard if not impossible to surrender the pride of a sharp mind. But the mind can only lead you to the brink of the precipice. To jump off requires the grace of love. Love, like the divine, is beyond the categories of good and bad. In the form of Shiva, it can behave in a wild and unpredictable manner, for it is like fire that consumes the chaff of mental churning and reduces the ore of our individuality to the gold at the kernel of our being.

Sathya Sai's adoption of the role of Shirdi Baba has been complete and unwavering from the day of its annunciation. It is clear that from the very start of his mission, Sathya Sai was in no doubt about his unusual status that apparently combines the role of a dynamic Sufi saint (who theoretically does not reincarnate) with that of a Hindu brahmachari. The differences in the attitude and behaviour of Shirdi Sai and Sathya Sai are undeniable but not irreconcilable. Puttaparthi Sai has explained the difference in emphasis by likening the two incarnations to a mother preparing food. She gets angry if her children interrupt her work just as Shirdi did. But when she serves the food the mother is more loving, like Sathya Sai. As a *kalandar* (Sufi mendicant), Shirdi Baba could not afford to be choosy in his diet or dress, while Sathya Sai, because of his family connection, had to set the example of eschewing meat and stimulants. The only real difference is in their public image—the first a bizarre, colourful and unconventional ascetic, the second a low-key, staid and un-hippy-like semi-recluse. Whereas Sathya Sai extends a courteous welcome to all, the fakir could affront new arrivals with choice abuse and demand money from them, sometimes beyond their means.

One way to understand these often outrageous demands is to view them in the context of the Deccan Bhakti tradition within which the saints characteristically belonged to the lower castes and were unacquainted with wealth except at the spiritual level. There is irony in a mendicant testing the faith of well-to-do seekers who swear that God is more important to them than money. Shock treatment alone can break some people's ingrained notions about the nature of real religion. Gurdjieff's bizarre remedies, not unlike Basaveshwara's movement to reactivate the kernel of Shaivite devotion, relied on challenging the fossilized structure of society. In its day, the Lingayat revival was a revolutionary force in Karnataka (and parts of Andhra Pradesh). A vigorous people's movement that explored democratic ideas of equality between castes six hundred years ahead of its time, it shocked the brahminical order into a defensive posture and strengthened Dravidian cultural identity. The Sai

Parampara, by choosing to manifest and grow in backward village situations, is clearly on the side of the common cultivator. Its appearance, first in the torn robes of a scruffy fakir, and next in the deprived dress of a poor village boy, is evidence of its loyalty to the reformist vision of generations of Deccan teachers who stressed that true religion is beyond caste, creed or social status.

The coming of Prema Sai, the third Sai Baba was first predicted by Sathya Sai in 1960. Apparently, Prema Sai's father is already living in Mandya district of Karnataka, whose son will declare himself only after the passing of Sathya Sai. So, while Shirdi Baba is assumed in the (orthodox) Puttaparthi lore to be Shiva, and Sathya Sai the joint manifestation of Shiva and Parvati, the third avatar represents Parvati alone. (Another version has it that Prema Sai will be born a Christian. Already portraits of the saint-to-be in the Puttaparthi bazaar cast him in the likeness of Christ. Unsurprisingly, to further its influence, the brahminising lobby has ingeniously predicted that Prema Sai would have, as mother, someone who in a former birth had been a brahmin.) Prema Sai's calling will be the unification of warring religions, thus completing the mission of his predecessors in Shirdi and Puttaparthi.

{9}

Hear Ye the Word

Puttaparthi Sai's voluminous output, in spoken and in printed form, crowds the shelves in dozens of Indian and foreign languages at the Prasanthi bookshop. Devotees buy these books not just to read, but as talismans to help bridge the desperate sense of loneliness their souls feel on leaving the presence of their teacher. It is baffling to the outsider to see the turnover of these titles that seem only to repeat what conventional religion has been propounding for centuries: 'Be good, do good, be aware of life's oneness, let your actions speak louder than words.' While Sai devotees hang on to Baba's every word printed (in monthly installments since 1958) in the ashram magazine *Sanathan Sarathi,* the ordinary reader finds Professor Kasturi's English renderings from the Telugu somewhat heavy-going. I find the translation too literal and, while some of the blame can be attributed to the flat landscape of the Saxon soul, the translator's sugary tone and flowery turn of phrase does not help. Educated readers in English find India's predilection for the mythic yawn-inducing anyway and the official versions of Sai Baba's writings, with their reluctance to edit out the far-fetched and make the story relevant to the cultural expectations of an enquiring audience, seem designed to keep them away. The narrative is allowed to become repetitious, banal and diffuse. Perhaps, as a former professor, the editor is sensitive to Baba's listing of scholarship as one of the nine deadly attributes of the ego!

What comes across to the modern reader of the dozen *Vahini* collections of Baba's monthly articles is their quaint tone reminiscent of Victorian morality. The fact is that these articles were written in the vernacular (Telugu), largely for a peasant audience. However, the style obscures much of the wisdom, provided both in textual exegesis and practical hints to the devotee. When read in the original, as part of *Sanathan Sarathi* where they appear amidst other ashram opinions and happenings (including medical miracles), these writings astonish with their range and depth. Baba effortlessly describes the subtleties distinguishing the Hindu philosophical schools in a few sentences, so casually that it suggests total mastery of the field. This mastery extends from Hindu philosophy to Hindu custom and he relates in considerable detail (for example) the penitent lifestyle a *vanaprastha* (retired householder) is expected to follow. Reading these expert comments on a wide range of subjects is rather like consulting an encyclopaedia of religion. Better than the theory of religion, however, is Baba's advice on the way to live, which is simple and effective: 'Cultivate love by two methods. Firstly, consider the faults of others, no matter how big, to be negligible. Consider your own faults, no matter how insignificant, to be big. Secondly, when you speak, remember God hears every word. Be aware of His omnipresence.'

From a perusal of the first year's *Sanathan Sarathi*, several valuable lessons can be imbibed. The first issue commemorates the Shivaratri festival in 1958. Baba describes life as a yagna and sleep as samadhi. Eating is a part of worship, he says, as is the gardener's growing of the flower that is offered for puja. The second issue gives Baba's guarantee: 'You are free to discard me but I will not discard you.' In the May issue of the same year, reference is made to the growing band of critics (referred to as 'hole-pickers') and Baba's measured response: 'Stones are only thrown at a tree laden with fruit, not at a barren stump.' In the next issue, he brings home how the Mahabharata, Ramayana and Gita are all enacted within each one of us. He stresses how the use of the correct word is important to get the right meaning. (An unintended example of this lesson is provided by the dictum 'Karma without bhakti is a wall without a basement. The word should have been 'foundation'!) Baba recommends in the November issue that we live on the 'third floor' (of our *sattvic* being) to avoid scorpion stings. In a powerful image, he likens the soul to a piece of charcoal that, when turned incandescent by fire, resembles the Paramatma.

One of Baba's earlier books, *Prasnottara Vahini*, is in the form of questions and answers and proves that while he does not insist on the paraphernalia of conventional religion, neither does he discourage it when it can be of help to somebody. He answers questions on the four ashramas, pancha kosas, moksha, karma, vidya, varna, mantra, japa, yoga and tapas. The discussion is succinct and objective, steering clear of controversy, as is Baba's style.

A collection of Baba's discourses, *Sathya Sai Speaks*,

compiled from notes taken by Kasturi, was published in
1962. It opens with a poem by the translator on Baba's
'tinkling, twinkling, tintinnabulating Telugu'. Fortunately,
Sathya Sai lacks the voice of the haranguer whose rhetoric,
by virtue of its ringing sound, distracts the hearer from
the fact that little if anything is being said. Baba is more
concerned with the meaning of his words getting across
and, while talking, becomes engrossed in making sure his
audience understands what he is trying to say. With his
flair for peasant humour, he has called his talks not feasts
for the ear but medicine for the mind. The word
'discourse', therefore, conveys better than 'lecture' his
attempt to treat a philosophic subject in a general way so
that all can understand. He describes his talks as an
opportunity for both him and his audience to share their
love, and usually begins and ends them with the singing
of Telugu verses.

The opening words of his series of discourses (that
now run to some thirty-five volumes dating back to
1953) state how clear and simple the way to know God
is: 'When I was at Uravakonda, studying in the High
School, I came away one day and threw away my books
and declared that I have My work waiting for Me. That
day, when I came out publicly as Sai Baba, the first song
I taught the gathering was:

Maanasa bhajare guru charanam
Dusthara bhava sagaratharanam

(Install the Lord in your heart and offer him your
thoughts, feelings and actions.)

In these words is summarized his public message: active
compassion performed in a mood of selfless devotion is

all that is required. Most of us ignore the reality that Sai Baba's store is filled with everything a person needs. We must stop cluttering the mind with unwanted furniture and ask Sai Baba to supply our essential needs. This particular discourse, delivered at the 1953 Dussehra celebrations held in Prasanthi, is extraordinary for its confident prediction of the exponential expansion of Sathya Sai's mission: 'Do not question how and whether I can do all this ... correcting the crookedness of the human mind and guiding humanity back to sanatan dharma.' Spelled out at the outset is the compassionate nature of his work: 'The wicked will not be destroyed ... they will be corrected and led back to the path from which they have strayed.' He ends with a caution: 'Having grown old and filled your heads with all kinds of doctrines and dogmas you now have to use your discrimination and discover God the hard way.'

The early discourses delivered before smaller audiences engender a more intimate atmosphere. By the Chitravati river, in February 1958, Baba talked about Seshagiri Rao, an unbeliever who was fascinated by the aura of the boy saint. One day in 1940, Baba had caught the man peeping into his prayer hall and invited him inside to 'examine' Sai Baba. Seshagiri Rao came in and stayed on. Baba uses this as an example of why he has come on earth—to sow the seeds of faith amongst the doubters. 'I do not insist that a person should have faith in God,' Baba says. 'Not even bhakti is essential. It is love, to expand one's heart to take in the whole of humanity.' Hence his preference for the title 'Premaswarupa' (image of love) both for himself and his audience. Baba also notes that the only difference between the theist and atheist is that they view the same tree from different angles.

In Madras the same year, Baba cautioned the gathering: 'Mention was made of Puttaparthi and you were advised to go there and draw inspiration from the bhajan. Please do not incur the expense. Whenever you call on me, your village can be made Puttaparthi.' Baba issued a further caution: 'Even in my case, do not be attracted simply by stories of what I create by a wave of the hand. Do not jump to conclusions with closed eyes; watch, study and weigh. Never yield unless you feel the inner satisfaction of being on the right path.' This advice to cultivate a scientific temper is often ignored by overenthusiastic devotees who feel that Sai Baba will think for them.

At Nellore he discusses his own mystery: 'The best you can do is to get immersed in it. Then you can discuss me to your heart's content.' At Mirthipadu he expresses his pleasure in being among farmers 'who are engaged in hardy toil and who sacrifice their personal comfort in order to make others happy'. At Peddapuram he confides, 'Understand yourself and that will reveal Me also.' Amongst the scholars at Venkatagiri he asserts, 'I know your profession and status. But you do not know mine. I am neither a Shastravadin nor a Buddhivadin. I am a Premavadin. So lay down the chopper of analysis and pick up the laddu of love.'

To a gathering of Sanskrit students he advised, 'The embodiment of love can only be understood through love. To grasp my meaning you have to fathom your own reality. Scholarship is only a means to mastership of the mind.' Back at Prasanthi after this tour of Andhra he found it necessary to correct certain misconceptions held by the bhaktas about his true nature. 'I am unaffected by karma. For me your joy is my food, your exhilaration the swing on which I sit. My task is to shower you with joy. I do not wish that you extol me. I shall be satisfied if you rely on me. I bring tears of joy and I wipe tears of grief. I make people mad for God and I cure those mad for ungodly things.'

In this sampling from spontaneous talks by Sai Baba at wayside halts to a variety of audiences (many of them unsophisticated) during tours of the Andhra countryside between 1958 and 1960, the dynamism of the man and his message can be sensed. Most religious speakers—and India seems to have lakhs of them just itching to get behind a microphone—donate little to the memory as token of their wisdom. Sathya Sai is otherwise and can always be relied on to leave a powerful impression by word or example. Significantly, people flock not to hear him but to be near him. This is India's unique acid test for determining a person's spiritual status. Beholding the divine in a person can, in rare cases, result in viewing a near-physical aura. Compared to this glory beheld by the inner eye, the words of a teacher seem of secondary importance. This is revealed when listening to Sathya Sai's discourses where a good part of the audience may not understand Telugu, his preferred medium. In spite of not comprehending his words, many can intuit his message—evidence, if any were needed, of the power of love to bridge the communication gap.

Inevitably, with such a voluminous number of discourses available for study, it is possible for critics to 'prove' almost anything about Sathya Sai. By selecting passages out of context they can show him to be a communist, capitalist, monarchist, republican, conservative, liberal, orthodox or non-conformist. This is another good reason for the sincere seeker to make the effort to have darshan and find out for himself who this remarkable presence really is.

In *Dharma Vahini* for example, Baba, who normally avoids any controversy or criticism of people or things, speaks strongly against women's lib and states most uncharacteristically: 'The educated woman is but a painted doll.' The strength of his feelings suggests this opinion dates back to his earlier social conditioning, before he saw the need to build a ladies' college at Anantapur. By neglecting to clarify this, the editor misleads readers into concluding that this is Sai Baba's current thinking on the subject. Similar and more serious examples of his seeming traditionalist mindset, made more outmoded by unimaginative translation, are allowed to misrepresent Sai Baba's early thoughts. In Baba's defence of the caste system, the translator clumsily asserts: 'If all feel there is but one varna, the welfare and security of the world will be endangered. If all command who obeys?' This wording gives ammunition to those looking for an excuse to criticize Sai Baba on the grounds of obscurantism. However, it is answered by Sai himself in the eighth issue of *Sanathan Sarathi* when he quotes Rama's graceful reply to the outcaste woman Sabari: 'My kinship is not of race or caste but of bhakti.'

Ramakatha Rasavahini is Baba's longest work to date, running to some 800 pages. While the Ramayana has undoubtedly been the most loved work in many parts of India, Kasturi's claim that 'no other story in human history has had such profound impact on the mind of man' may sound parochial to the rest of the world, which is not familiar with the Ramayana. Having at the outset declared Rama as the 'indweller, the reality of your existence and the very embodiment of dharma that holds mankind together in love', the editor manages by the end to bring these verities into dispute. He does not bother to tone down the feudal sentiments that come through in Rama's banishment of Sita. (There are, of course, other versions of the Ramayana that do not end in Sita's exile.) Since she appears in this instance to have been sentenced for being innocent, how can such injustice be passed off as a spiritual decision made from higher motives? It appears to contradict Baba's message that love is the nature of the divine and seems to toe the orthodox line that societal convenience comes before individual fulfilment. The universal aspect of Rama's personality, according to some scholars, has been deliberately narrowed down in this version of the Ramayana to suit brahminical requirements.

Baba's commentary was addressed to an earlier generation of Indian visitors to Puttaparthi who were familiar with the Hindu scriptures on which he chose to write his commentaries, the *Bhagavatha Vahini*, *Geetha Vahini*, *Dhyana Vahini*, *Prema Vahini* and the *Upanishad Vahini* among others. (Perhaps of all of Baba's writings, *Upanishad Vahini* is the most lucid. Each of the ten most famous Upanishads is described concisely and tellingly with such gems of insight as 'the universe is an instrument to reveal the majesty of God' and 'when the Atman is understood, all else is understood'.)

Such connotations are familiar and culturally meaningful to Indian ears, if not always acceptable to everyone. Even the average Indian, however, would be confused at Baba's mention, on the one hand, of how women are qualified to hear Hinduism's highest teaching (of '*Brahma jnana*') and, on the other, how they should consciously devalue themselves to worship their husbands as God. Today, one of India's chief sources of pride is the advanced knowledge of information technology that makes it a leading player in this field in the world. Bangalore, where Baba has an ashram, is Asia's IT capital and educated Indian women are among its most brilliant success stories. It is unfortunate that the context of Baba's earlier statements is not clarified. No attempt is made to convey Baba's modern interests.

Sathya Sai's early speeches also convey a zealous attempt to stand up for ancient India's spiritual heritage. While spending a night at Swami Shivananda's ashram at Rishikesh in 1960 (the year Sathya Sai passed through en route to Badrinath), I remember how a simple sadhu lecturing on Indian culture spoke of the aeroplane having been invented by the rishis in Vedic times. This need to upstage modern western science by referral to ancient genius may signify some compensatory salvaging of pride after the colonial experience. Sathya Sai clearly shares the sadhu's spirited defence of ancient India's genius. In his inaugural address to the world conference of his service organizations, Baba makes several pointed references to what he considers the 200 years of alien influence of British colonialism. He appears unconcerned that his own Andhra heritage for the last 2,800 years has been at the receiving end of Aryan cultural colonialism. A minor but telling detail lies in Baba's observation that 'Sanskrit is the parent and core of all languages'. Possibly the translator has been too literal because any student of linguistics knows that Sanskrit is only the parent of the Indo-European group of languages. It is not even the parent of Baba's own tongue, Telugu, let alone of the languages of the Far East, the Americas or Africa. Scientifically speaking, English is a true-blooded offspring of Sanskrit while Telugu is only a foster child in the process of adoption.

Baba's zeal to promote the cause of ancient India's genius leads him to advance the somewhat staggering claim that in 3043 BCE an Indian yogi had predicted the departure of the British from India. Assuming this to be true, the claim suggests dismay that India's spiritual purity had been sullied by foreign material influences. (It is thought that the popular Indian term for disgust at a foreign 'contaminator'—*mleccha*—may have derived from an ancient tribe of traders.) According to another observation made by Baba at the first All India Conference of his Seva organizations in Madras, 'It is only after the advent of the East India Company that the struggle for political power predominated.' The East India Company received its charter half a century after the collapse of Vijayanagar and, whatever its sins committed for commercial greed, it did not sacrifice the lives of slaves in the name of religion as did the greatest of the Vijayanagar emperors, Krishnadeva Raya. (Ironically, it was one of the Vijayanagar vassals from Sathya Sai's neighbouring province who first sold land to the British to enable them to gain a physical foothold in India.)

Sai Baba's initial glorification of India's past and the recounting of the greatness of Hinduism's antiquity seem at odds with his teaching that we should not take undue

Shirdi Sai Baba with attendants late in his life.

The young Sathya Sai Baba being felicitated at a devotee's home in the days before his own ashram was built in Puttaparthi.

Early portrait of Sathya Sai Baba taken at a devotee's home in Bangalore.

Sai Baba with his pet dogs
Tommy and Henry.

Sai Baba being
garlanded on his
birthday by Sai Geeta,
his pet elephant in
Puttaparthi.

In 1952 the young Sathya Sai Baba drives a car
loaned by a devotee.

Sai Baba performing a puja at Somnath.

Sai Baba trekking the Himalayas en route to Badrinath in 1961.

Sai Baba with the Governor of Uttar Pradesh's party during
the Badrinath yatra.

Sai Baba in Hardwar prior to his Badrinath yatra.

Sai Baba overseeing the construction work at his Prasanthi Nilayam campus. Unusually, he is seen wearing sandals.

In the Jamnagar palace of the late Rajmata of Jamnagar.

Crowds of lady devotees strain to catch a glimpse of
Sathya Sai Baba on a visit to Shimla.

At a yagna being performed by Vedic pundits at Venkatagiri.

During the Shivaratri celebration of Vibhuti Abishek at Prasanthi
Nilayam. Sacred ash cascades over an image of Shirdi Sai from
the empty upturned pot held by Prof. Kasturi, as Sathya Sai Baba
vigorously scours its interior.

With a group of student musicians at Jamnagar, Gujarat.

Listening to bhajans at the future site of his
Whitefield ashram near Bangalore.

Walking amidst enthusiastic crowds on
the streets of Dharwad in Karnataka.

Travelling in a procession in an open jeep in Andhra Pradesh.

Sai Baba giving darshan from his summer guesthouse in Kodaikanal, Tamil Nadu. He is holding letters from devotees in his hand.

Sai Baba's mother Easwaramma anointing his hair during his 36th birthday celebrations in 1962.

Feeding deer at Whitefield ashram in 1980.

For the past fifty years Sathya Sai Baba has been
giving darshan on special occasions from the balcony
of the Prasanthi Nilayam mandir.

In front of his former Prasanthi Nilayam residence. This open area
has since been covered to make the Sai Kulwant hall.

Enjoying a joke with students
during the annual sports meet
at the stadium in Puttaparthi.

Prithwi, Maharani of Jind (Rani-ma)
with Sri Sathya Sai Baba
in Kodaikanal in 2002.

The second convocation of the Sri Sathya Sai Institute of Higher Learning
held in the Purnachandra auditorium in Puttaparthi.
Madhuri Shah, chairman of the University Grants Commission was
the guest of honour.

In the blessing mode during daily darshan.

The super-specialty hospital at Puttaparthi.

The super-specialty hospital at Whitefield, Bangalore.

pride in our own caste, country or religion. This pride may reflect modern India's post-colonial search for a national identity. But if Hinduism's pride in its insights into the ever-present nature of our divine self is justified, why harp on the past? Sathya Sai uses the concept of 'sanatan dharma' in an idealistic sense, as the basis of all religion and morality, unlike the world at large which sees it as the fount of Hindu orthodoxy. In the same way, Baba suggests that because Sanskrit is the parent of the profoundest spiritual insights, this confers on it the symbolic status of mother of all languages. Again, the editor has not troubled to disentangle the different meanings the teacher and his audience might attach to such terms.

Later speeches are more true to Baba's message of universal appreciation of India's and the world's diverse cultures and suggest that his mission had got wise to those who tried to take advantage of his teachings. It is reasonable to assume that with his increasing fame and exposure to more sophisticated minds, early opinions culled from orthodox sources were suitably modified. Education is a tool that broadens the mind by removal of its narrow childhood conditioning. A university education may not bring a man nearer to God but it can carry his understanding from the provincial to the universal. Contact with foreign devotees would certainly have apprised Baba that spiritual yearning is not the monopoly of the Indian soul.

The reconciliation of early chauvinist opinions with later universalising philosophy can be understood if you view Sathya Baba in both, his orthodox and unorthodox manifestations. Until he built up his base amongst the orthodox he could not hope to expand to less orthodox audiences. It is only now (in the ashram diary for 2004) that Baba openly asserts that his essential being is not Hindu: 'I have not come to speak on behalf of any dharma like the Hindu dharma.' His twenty-first-century utterances suggest that he has moved beyond the Vedic just as he had earlier moved beyond the Sufic and Agamic. Unlike so many religious reformers, he is a conservative who takes good care not to throw out the baby with the bathwater. As a canny son of the soil, he realizes there is meaning in and use for everything. Some may read into this the preparing of the ground for the impending third avatar, Prema Sai, whose mission will be the unity of religions.

Fashions change even in religion. A generation ago, orthodox Hindus would think twice before crossing the kala pani. Today, pundits and pujaris are exported to perform Hindu pujas for expatriates round the world. Baba has said, 'I do not concern myself with these [fashionable activities] of the present-day world.' This is borne out by his indifference to all forms of media. For his seventy-fifth birthday, Baba was gifted a World Space channel which beams out crystal-clear digital radio programmes round the clock from satellites positioned above Singapore. The channel is called 'Sai Global Harmony' and while it brings delight to the ears of old devotees, to the world at large it seems to lack professionalism. Yet, there is immaculate professionalism on view everyday at the ashram, especially in the theatrical productions that take place routinely

Contradictions likewise appear in his printed works. For example, a chapter on 'one-pointedness' (as an aid to meditation) will leap bewilderingly from subject to subject and this darting about in chase of generalities seems hardly conducive to the build-up of concentration. The reason for this change of subject may be to retain his audience's interest since the bigger the audience, the harder it is to keep their ear. Sai Baba's discourses—at least in translation—can seem diffuse in the themes they cover and it is rare for any single theme to monopolize the session. With a mixed audience of some ten to twenty thousand devotees of different backgrounds, interests and expectations, Baba has to try and appeal to them all and this may account for the random switching of subject and direction of argument.

Whatever the devotees may feel about Baba's talents as a speaker and a writer, the rest of the world judges his words objectively and concludes that his expression must be commensurate with his education. What makes sense to the student of religion but may seem blasphemous to the narrow-minded among Baba's followers, is the reasonable assumption that any avatar who enjoys the best of both worlds (i.e. his humanity is supplemented with superhuman inputs carried over from the divine realm) is unlikely to foster any real change in the world. In order to be effective in appealing to human hearts, the avatar must be fully human, temporarily suppressing his divine glory. If he (or she) does not face the same physical, mental and spiritual challenges as the average human being, the example of divine love will go in vain. The lesson of Baba's life on earth is not that he came trailing clouds of glory but, instead, was born without frills in a tough, discouraging environment which he had to overcome by dint of self-discipline. It is noticeable in

Baba's discourses of the late 1960s how a note of disappointment has crept in over the performance of volunteers for whom, ten years earlier, he had held high hopes. Perhaps they felt that Baba, would invoke the fullness of divinity and smile on their shortcomings. Out of his divinely commissioned compassion, he would do all their work for them.

It follows from the above assumption that Baba is bound by the same physical and mental (though not necessarily spiritual) laws as the rest of humanity and, while his recall of divine wisdom is unique to him, in matters of mundane learning his development can only be commensurate with his schooling. For example, his English is of the local variety and his pronunciation and vocabulary are derived from his experience as a village schoolboy. Aspects of the village youth's experience would colour to some extent the outlook of the avatar (or whatever) and most likely influence his expression. This theory at least would explain some contradictory positions.

What it does not explain however is his apparent repertoire of higher spiritual learning despite lack of formal schooling and education. Stories about his linguistic abilities suggest that he has unusual sympathies. He intuits from the foreign devotees' body language what they are trying to say. Outside his familiarity with Telugu and kindred southern vernaculars, Baba shares the itinerant holy man's lingua franca of Hindustani and a basic command of English, free of any idiomatic colouring. His knowledge of Sanskrit is more puzzling and seems, on occasion, to derive directly from a source other than books. Ramana Maharishi was considered to have a surprisingly deep knowledge of Sanskrit given that he had run away to his holy mountain as a schoolboy. However, all his life he was discussing abstruse philosophy with his disciples and his knowledge of Sanskrit could have come from the books that were consulted during these encounters. But that could only happen in an orthodox ashram setting. Sathya Sai has neither had the opportunity nor the inclination to take lessons, so the source of his knowledge of Hindu texts remains baffling. It is hard to explain how—when the occasion demands—he seems to have access to a store of higher knowledge. Kasturi recounts how he had once gone to ask Baba for a chapter on the Brihadaranyaka Upanishad (the longest of the Upanishads) for inclusion in the next issue of *Sanathan Sarathi* and Baba kept him waiting only twenty minutes while he dashed off, in hand-written Telugu, a twenty-page article that is a remarkable résumé of this most difficult Upanishad. Just as baffling is the prodigious nature of his output of Telugu hymns. When he was still young he had composed nine hundred bhajans which were written by hand in a notebook. (Curiously, the pages were numbered in Arabic.)

Baba may continually call attention to the risks inherent in pride of learning and the danger of argumentativeness acquired from reading books, but the fact remains that he sees education as a crucial part of his mission. For all his fulsome praise of ancient India, the fact is that learning then was confined to the priestly class. From the outset Baba aims to provide education across the spectrum of society. Critics who suggest he has limited familiarity with worldly subjects need to remember that he put his mission before the completion of his education. Dropping out of school as a teenager deprived Baba of the opportunity to sharpen what was clearly an outstanding intellect. Baba's formal horizons were fixed at the level of rural Telugu culture with its experience of life drawn largely from the Hindu scriptures and the unspoken need for their defence from any modern probing. The absence of higher studies should have deprived him of the ability to keep abreast of current investigations on the frontiers of science yet, extraordinarily, he personally prescribes research projects at the cutting edge of modern technology for his postgraduate students.

The difference between a half-schooled mind and an educated one is akin to the difference in the quality of light that a window lets in, depending on how clean it is. One proof of the freedom that comes with higher education is in the absence of absolutes in one's outlook. It is the person of limited learning, with strong convictions based on half-understood premises, who adopts extreme positions and rigid regimens. This is often tinged with an edge of anti-carnal scorn, implying that the divine source of life has somehow slipped up in vouchsafing such mysteries to irresponsible mankind.

Such guilt-driven and life-negating attitudes may be a feature of many orthodox Indian ashrams but the Prasanthi campus, thanks to Sai Baba's joy-affirming doctrine, is free of this hangover. Segregation of male and female devotees is based on a practical and sensible assessment of reality. While Sai Baba himself encourages the delights of existence and in private interviews proves most sympathetic to a broad-minded view of life, the visitor still gets the feeling that some Puttaparthi devotees lack a vigorous appreciation of the beauty of the mind. In championing the supremacy of the heart they tend to play down the divine credentials of a shining intellect.

10

In Tune with the Infinite

Those who seek a formal presentation of the teachings of the Sai Parampara, whether of the Shirdi or Puttaparthi dispensation, are dismayed when referred to either *Shri Sai Satcharita* or *Sai Vahini*, both of which are rambling anecdotal accounts rather than any systematic formulations. However, a steady perusal of these devotional treatises will prove to be richly rewarding. Sathya Sai had once recommended a thorough reading of the *Srimad Bhagavat* to Diana Baskin, saying that the essence of his love would be found in it. Setting aside a week, she went through this devotional text from beginning to end. The exercise proved to be the spiritual highlight of her life. The point about getting involved with any of these books is that, absorbed by the mood they engender, the soul registers more than the mind.

The morality and doctrine of the Sai religion derive more from the devotee's parent religion than from any new code. The Deccan saints did not come to establish a new religion but to water the roots of the old and give them new life. Sai Baba's teachings exist to intensify and universalize the teachings of our hearth, activating love wherever it manifests. According to Sathya Sai, 'I have no plans to attract disciples or devotees into my fold or any fold. I have come to tell you of this universal unitary faith, this path of love.' Like Shirdi Baba he does not want us to desert our ancestral faith. He wants that we become true Hindus, real Muslims and Christ-like Christians. The idea is not to think with the head, but to see with the heart the simple truth that divinity is the same as humanity. To strengthen this perception we need to pay less importance to the impedimenta of formal religion. Instead, we should perform service to mankind. Sai's mission urges us to stop being a wiseacre about God and recognize him in our next-door neighbour. True religion lies not in clasping both hands in prayer towards a distant deity but in extending one hand in compassion to the needy soul next door.

For the student of theology a visit to Puttaparthi can be revealing. Many people who have had no concern with religion in their lives experience the plenitude of divinity when they confront Baba and, through love, they know intuitively that which took theologians centuries to work out. The critical factor is the presence of Sathya Sai Baba. Then all questions about whether the upper descends to bless the lower or the lower rises to fulfil the upper, or whether God is man realized or man is God miniaturized, become immaterial. All mental chattering is stilled in the fullness of the heart's certainty.

For some it is disconcerting to find that Sathya Sai eschews all trappings of religion. His striking orange robe seems to reflect the sun's warming propensities—the very opposite of the colour of renunciation. On his birthday and at Christmas he favours a white robe. During Dussehra it may be maroon. Nitpickers have criticized some of the materials used as being too flashy according to the ancient canons of what the well-dressed holy man should wear. They ignore the possibility that to his followers Sathya Sai is no less than the Grand Designer and hence has every right to determine the fashions. The robe is stitched by the village tailor and is washed by a Puttaparthi dhobi. The old robes are presented to favoured disciples and are treasured, in the Indian tradition, as family heirlooms.

A visit to Puttaparthi can also be unsettling to an intellectual who goes expecting to find just another holy man when, in fact, what he finds—but often fails to see— is something infinitely grander. Only the soul prepared for the full vision is vouchsafed the grace of finding love embodied in this slight frame. And when you have love, who needs religion or anything else? This is the ultimate high for the seeker. Beyond this, ecstasy cannot go. For the soul in search of itself, here at Puttaparthi (or Shirdi) the wine of the spirit can be drunk neat and neither priest nor ritual clutters the landscape. His temple is made up of the body of his devotees. His religion is their devotion to the love he arouses.

For the Sai teaching, in a nutshell, is the need to experience love. Its underlying mantra has been enunciated by Shirdi Baba in the phrase *Sab ka Malik Ek*, because it is this feeling of oneness that love bestows. The revolutionary relocation of the divine from a stern external figure to a compassionate witness within devolves moral responsibility on each devotee. He is forced to acknowledge that what he sees in Sai is not just love personified but personalized. In his divinized being we can behold the goal of human oneness, the prefect marriage of male and female in a single body, the only sure promise of peace on earth. The crux of the Sai faith lies in partaking of love's holy communion where loyalty to our ancestral religion is transcended by the experience of oneness. It recognizes the value of outer religion as the vehicle by which we arrive at the doors of love's infinite perception. Shirdi Baba addressed this moment of dual identity when he faced his fellow Muslims who were agitated by the idea of Hindus offering worship to a human being in a mosque. Shirdi did not deny that monotheistic norms were being transgressed, but he appealed to the Muslim critics to understand the lofty motivation of the Hindus in worshipping a mleccha in a mosque, thereby transgressing their own dharmic norms. By accepting the worship not for his body but for the inner spirit, he was demonstrating that love alone is the miracle that turns the water of religion into the wine of the spirit.

Love of our fellow men, irrespective of their religious affiliation, confirms our true identity as spiritual beings. Conventional religion provides false documents and makes us believe that our 'home address' is with some church or sect when, in fact, it is 'c/o the divine, at the feet of suffering humanity'. The Buddha discovered this truth but his religion was stifled in the subcontinent by those who found feudal hierarchy a more profitable option. Mahatma Gandhi likewise preached a compassionate message that some elements of the same orthodox lobby found disadvantageous. While most are depressed by the way the custodians of public faith betray and distort the teaching of their founders, the Sai Parampara, anchored

as it is in the divine nature of love, has never been unduly
disturbed by these dismal realities. Throughout his mission,
Sathya Sai has displayed a supreme confidence in his
works and, like Christ, never wavered in the face of
carping critics and their vilifying reports. The state of the
world is the Almighty's problem: you and I need only
concern ourselves with a compassionate regard for life
wherever its miraculous manifestation crosses our path.

It is true that some devotees at both places have
drawn up their own code of personal behaviour and
believe that by following it they win Sai Baba's special
grace. But this is a voluntary scheme and, since it ensures
a practical means of maintaining the peace and the
orderly functioning of the huge ashram at Puttaparthi, it
has won Sathya Sai's approval. These Seva Dal devotees,
as they are called, agree to a minimum programme of Sai
devotion and social service which, if sincerely followed,
grants them the opportunity to join in the running of the
campus when it is their particular state organization's
turn to do so. This sometimes confers boring and menial
duties—and the more testing task of crowd control—to
the volunteers but also gives them the rare privilege of
being guaranteed Sathya Sai's darshan and blessings at
the end. This arrangement is particularly suitable for
poor devotees who would otherwise not be able to afford
to spend a prolonged period in Puttaparthi.

Because of Sai's single-pointed focus on arousing love,
he is more concerned that his teaching is absorbed by the
heart rather than the head. Analyse love and you kill it.
The problem in expressing the fullness of love's teaching
in English lies in its frustrating lack of a spiritual
vocabulary. Nowhere do we find any signs of Saxon

awareness that a man is real apart from his body. The idea of an individual soul is respected but, considered seemingly irrelevant to everyday affairs, is not pursued to its logical end. That leaves us with the awkward use of 'self' which is one of most poorly considered words in the entire lexicon. The in-fashion phrase 'self-actualization' conjures up excruciating exercises for something as simple as yoga. How does one convey the mystery of the unseen mystical being at the heart of the universe? How does one relate this cosmic vision to the undying flame of selfhood within our own heart? The term *consciousness* poses such a challenge to the Englishman that he rarely bothers to think about it. Even the word *God* is a challenging assignment best left for a Sunday morning when, traditionally, there has been no getting away from Him!

*

One issue that confronts a student of religion in a study of Sathya Sai is that of avatarhood, which although central to Christian doctrine is basically a Hindu concept. The issue needs to be addressed since, as has already been mentioned, many disciples view the Sai Parampara as a manifestation of the avatar principle. This study suggests that Sri Sathya Sai has no equal (that the author is aware of) in the entire history of religion when it comes to combining simple living with a phenomenal and sustained radiation of a spiritual aura which, in turn, has translated into an array of good works. Here, for the first time on earth, we have it seems the exciting prospect of a manifestation of what is truly divine, not man and spirit in theoretically equal parts, but both fully embodied to reveal life's ultimate mystery, the real nature of love. Throughout history we have only had the word of prophets, teachers and messengers as to how God, as pure spirit, is believed to behave. The Buddha and Mahavir achieved the equivalent of divine status through penance, while Jesus appears to enjoy divine status with retrospective effect, having had divinity conferred on him by a succession of church councils. Shirdi Sai was not worshipped as the Godhead until some years after his passing whereas Sathya Sai, from the age of fourteen, has been regarded as divinity incarnate. (Some devotees read special significance into the fact that, two days before Sathya Sai's birth, Sri Aurobindo had interrupted a prolonged vow of silence to announce the birth of an infallible power that would kindle immortal fire in earthly hearts and whose voice would be heard by the multitude.)

Mainstream Vaishnav doctrine holds that ten avatars (which vary according to local tradition) are foretold, the most complete of them being Krishna's, who fulfils the sixteen attributes that mark the perfect divine descent. According to Dr Gokak (*In Defence of Jesus Christ and Other Avatars*, 1979), other sects, including the Shaivite, also posit avatars and these vary in power and presence. For example, a less endowed avatar is referred to as 'Vibhuti' and souls of great attainment, like Shankaracharya and Vivekananda, can (according to Sri Aurobindo) be likened to these.

The only problem with avatar status is that it limits Sathya Sai to a sectarian concept of divinity while, to most devotees, his divine attributes appear to be of universal application. This person stands above and beyond all doctrine and, like the overruling atman, though closer to each one of us than our own heart, is beyond definition or description. People who limit Baba to the role of an avatar may be taking the easy option that closes the mind to even greater wonders that this person embodies. If, as seems on occasion likely, Sathya Sai embodies the very nature of the divine, calling him an avatar is mistaking the finger that points to the moon for the moon itself. What comes across to me is that we have, in Sri Sathya Sai Baba, the universal soul in Hindu dress, the full effulgence of divine love contracted into the span of a lowly Andhra villager.

It took Christians centuries of rancorous argument before sophisticated churchmen could arrive at a formula to describe the grandeur of Christ's being. The church was at pains to thrash out a compromise solution to explain a tricky mystery and could only come up with a loveless formula that satisfied the most fastidious of nitpicking intellectuals: 'The Son of God is consubstantial with the Father in Godhead and with us in manhood, the distinctive character of each person being preserved.' For the next thousand years Christendom was terrorized to toe this doctrinal line. The alternative was death—for the good of one's soul. Upanishadic freedom of thought was unthinkable under these circumstances. Contrast this delayed and contentious assessment with the immediate acknowledgment of divinity by the peasants of Rayalseema. Certain of their own spiritual insights, they promptly accorded their young prophet full honour in his own land. Such remarkable testimony to the discrimination of the Deccan villager invariably gets overlooked in the history of religion.

Sathya Sai has spelled out the purpose of an avatar:

'To protect dharma, his devotees, the Vedas and those who recite them.' This traditional agenda, couched in orthodox terms, clearly dates back to the early days of his mission. Two generations later, Chaitanya Jyoti's seven-layered structure symbolically reveals how the concept of avatar has blossomed from the traditional to the universal. Now Sai's unconquerable outflow of love is revealed as the chaitanya (consciousness) that motivates the divine play of the cosmos. For this reason, crowning a commemorative Chinese stupa is not a sphere, representing the world, but an oval, balanced on a finger which points to the feeling of wonder of all who gaze heavenwards in rapture, as they contemplate the glory of its great architect.

According to Hindu tradition (especially Vaishnav) there are six recognizable qualities in a full avatar: splendour, beauty, wealth, wisdom, fame and detachment. Puttaparthi devotees take pride in claiming for their Swami another modern attribute, and refer to him as 'the scientific avatar'. This is because he cautions people to examine and experience for themselves instead of accepting any teacher or message blindly. If the avatars of the north are represented as rulers of Dwarka and Ayodhya, the Sai avatar of the south is lord of the inner witness, a study in spiritual grace rather than kingly power. Whereas Krishna is depicted in upper India as the charioteer, dispensing hard knowledge of the human soul, in the Deccan he stands peasant-like, as at Pandharpur, dignifying in the form of Vitthal the dharma of ordinary mortals and available to the least of devotees who has love in his heart. Can we detect in these different emphases the working out of the ancient north–south struggle for cultural supremacy? Shirdi and Sathya Sai seem to stand halfway, seeking to reconcile these orthodox and protestant emphases, not yielding on their divine right to stay in touch with the ordinary, no matter how much the established hierarchy seeks to fit them into its pantheon. Professor Kasturi has shrewdly commented that Sathya Sai is the only avatar with a 'horizonless dimension, personifying spontaneous liberality of grace and unquestioning compassion for the foolish and fumbling'.

*

Physically, Sathya Sai has the slender but sturdy build of the south Indian ryot. Only five-feet-four in height, his presence is visibly enlarged by the grace of his bearing. Slim of hip by reason of a lifelong restrained diet, his shoulders are strong and even suggestive of some numinous overhang of psychic wings. This charge of psychic energy is seen in his gaze and, again, in the fluidity of his lips. It is almost as if his physical form is propelled by an inner grace that he is forced to rein in. The eyes are soft with compassion but, above them, a fold of skin between the eyebrows hints at a hidden power that tradition associates with the third eye. A prominent mole can be seen on his left cheek. The facial features share local traits but the eyes are boundless in their wonder. They often wear a soft, faraway look. Softly maternal one moment they can flash commandingly the next, as beautiful and unpredictable as the weather in the high mountains of Shivalaya. Like all masters he looks for the inner motive and this requires a penetrating gaze that can be disconcerting for many human hearts. A characteristic hand gesture that goes with this dreamlike expression is to write with a finger on the ether as though signifying that one's destiny has already been written. Another feature while walking before the daily gathering is to wipe his hands and face with white cotton handkerchiefs constantly replenished by his attendants, a sign to some of the active psychic ingredient at work through him.

So intriguing is Sathya Sai's psychic impact that the physical details tend to get blurred. To some his complexion is golden like the sun, while to others it resembles the sacred hue worn by other avatars, a blueish tinge that signifies the infinite. (When threading a *japa mala* [prayer beads] the devotee will avoid using this colour which is reserved for the divine beadsman.) When he walks, Sathya Sai is the personification of grace. His feet in themselves transmit his message of honouring the simple things of the earth and of becoming one with all around you. Western religion has lost the strange alchemy that the human foot can arouse. India has preserved it and is aware that the feet can be the means through which grace can flow. Western visitors to India are immediately alive to the contrast between the heavy tread of their own memsahibs and the gazelle-like motion of Asian ladies. Grace is essentially a feminine quality and Sathya Sai's physical presence betrays this soft aspect along with a magisterial air as he walks.

The characteristic hair style that crowns (much less so now that he is in his late seventies) his face is an adaptation of the local tendency towards frizzy hair. Early photographs show different styles. When Rani-ma first met Sathya Sai, he bent his head forward and anticipating her question said, 'It's real. You can pull it.' Prasanthi Nilayam is probably unique in the insistence of its master that the devotees must at all times be freshly bathed and cleanly turned out in simple but spruce attire. This is to honour the inner spirit which, contrary to conventional thought, is not indifferent to our appearance. Sathya Sai has learned the value of military discipline to keep devotees alive to their calling. The ashram routine may not appear to be physically severe but it can be punishing on those accustomed to easy-going habits.

Baba has pared down his own comforts to a bare minimum. His pokey quarters, attached to the mandir where he lived until the murderous attack in 1993, house only a bed and a table. The table will be strewn with devotees' letters, each of which merits some scrutiny, though Sathya Sai, it is said, can pick out those that require his immediate intervention.

The daily routine of Sathya Sai is an open book and has hardly varied in more than half a century. Like Shirdi Baba he has no personal belongings. The Buddha and Christ owned nothing between them and when my guru Sri Krishna Prem passed away, his worldly belongings amounted to a spare set of sannyasi's robes. Yet, possessing nothing, Sathya Sai is in command of funds most millionaires can only dream of. His treasure lies in his devotees to whom he is always available. However, with the huge increase in numbers have come security concerns and, yearly, the physical contact is shrinking, except for daily darshans.

His day starts at 3 a.m. when, after the morning bath and shave (using modern gizmos), he engages with the spirit, lapsing into the mode of self-awareness. At 6.30 a.m. he appears for darshan, having returned to the mode of out-turned maya. The magic of his presence illustrates part of the meaning of maya, which is usually translated as 'illusion'. It also means 'limited' and suggests a glimpse of an exquisite pattern in an unrolled tapestry. This is the role of an avatar, to reveal in the confined space of a human body the cosmic grandeur of life's informing spirit.

Almost always darshan is followed by bhajan. The singing of what in English is called hymns fails to do justice to the feelings of love that are invested in these songs. The crowds are at one with their teacher in the singing and he often leads them with what seems a professional ear. Traditionally, great store has been set by bhajan in the Bhakti tradition for it is the poor man's means to contact God directly without the intermediary of a priest. At festivals, Puttaparthi sees 'akhand bhajan', the non-stop, all-night singing of bhajans and these occasions arouse a frenzy of devotion. Sathya Sai is particular in supervising these energies to see that they do not get out of hand.

While bhajans are being sung, Sathya Sai chooses individuals, apparently at random, for an interview. Sometimes a larger group crowds into the small functional room on the ground floor of the mandir building. For an hour Baba relates informally and questions his visitors, often surprising them with his unexpected understanding of what they hold dear. At 9.30 a.m. he adjourns for his main meal of the day which is prepared by his family in the village, and is supplemented by dishes from old and close devotees. The meal is that satisfying south Indian institution, a vegetarian thali—a stainless steel tray with *katoris* (bowls) or compartments for a variety of small helpings of several different dishes. Unlike the north

Indian thali which will be heavy with oil, the southern is light and digestible. Sai Baba eats little, even of his favourite dishes, and prefers local tastes in the matter of vegetables and chutneys. His life has been characterized by an easy mastery over his tongue and items like potatoes, paan and coffee that he once enjoyed were relinquished on health grounds without any fuss. The strict, self-imposed discipline since childhood has given him control of the senses.

Till 11.30 a.m. Sathya Sai rests, and in silence enjoys his sole worldly activity of going through the morning newspaper. Needless to say, he prefers the Telugu-language press. (Ramana Maharishi also skimmed through the daily newspaper, his preference being for Tamil.) Otherwise, his only access to breaking news of the worldly kind is from his attendants. Sathya Sai employs no secretary and writes his own letters, articles for *Sanathan Sarathi*, signs cheques as chief trustee of the ashram funds and supervises every detail of the day-to-day administration of his expanding campus. At 12.30 he may have a snack of idli or dosa and this is followed by private time and lapse into the oceanic mode of silence. For India, the noisiest and most clangorous of countries, Prasanthi Nilayam comes as a blissful haven of peace. Darshan likewise is a memorable excursion into pin-drop silence where the intake of breath and the flutter of pigeons' wings are the only sounds to be heard.

By 3 p.m. the queuing lines of devotees are alive with expectation and in the afternoon darshan Sathya Sai mingles with the devotees, especially giving time to his students. He may collect letters, hand out presents or relax, listening to a music recital. This could range from classical Carnatic to Dixieland jazz and both find an appreciative ear in this universal master of harmony. After bhajans are sung at 5.30 p.m. Sathya Sai repairs for exercise, usually brisk walking before taking his light evening meal of chapattis and sabji prepared by his cooks. Then at 6.30 p.m. he retires from public view but not from work. More letters await his perusal and each one will be examined. So great is the volume that shredding has to be resorted to at the end of each day to make room for the next day's inflow.

For the devotee the highlight of the darshan may have been watching the simple act of Baba striking a match to light a puja lamp or breaking an auspicious coconut. What a fund of elegant grace Sathya Sai brings to such natural actions so pregnant with symbolism. Some may recall the whiff of fragrant vibhuti or even perfume that, in the tradition of Shirdi Baba, the saint of Puttaparthi enjoys. Grace, as a physical happening, is in evidence all the time when Baba is in residence. His unscheduled appearance, to visit one of his institutions or to meet an ailing disciple or a family member, can spark off a moment of blessing that seems to thrill the whole neighbourhood. The magic words 'Sai Baba has come' have only to be whispered and it spreads like wildfire as crowds are drawn towards his presence dropping whatever they may be doing.

*

Sai has come to open the third eye of love and his physical presence has the inherent grace to bring forth an understanding of such mysteries. Though cut in the image of soft femininity his mood is of masterfulness. Grace is not vouchsafed to the undeserving. The divine in human form is a paradox and, to emphasize its baffling possibilities, Sai Baba can say to his devotees, 'I am your property. I have no rights.' For a seeker, the Puttaparthi experience veers from outward single-minded focus on one person to the inner struggle to establish the truth of that undying presence within. The battle against the mind's doubting is fought a hundred times daily and lost—only to be won back briefly at darshan. But slowly the ocean of love reclaims the sandy shore of the devotee's doubts. The tidal conflict will continue but, one day, the devotee finds firm ground beneath his feet. The waves continue to wash over him but he is not swept away.

The realization dawns that Sathya Sai can only be recognized as divine because of the devotee's own capacity to achieve this state. The idea that Sai Baba is an avatar remains a theory until it dawns upon us that every soul is an avatar in the making. Nisarga Datta Maharaj succinctly states (in *I Am That*) that each of us is God though we don't know it. We suffer because of this ignorance of our real being. The inner task is to readjust our perception and realize, no matter how improbable it may seem, that there is no difference between Sai Baba and ourselves. Both Sai Babas exemplify the evolution of the human spirit to a level where it has transcended the demands of physical desire without denying its place in the scheme of things. Their lives (along with those of other saints who showed different paths) demonstrate the attainment of an ineffable state, beyond labels like avatar which limit them to the norms of sectarian religion. Shirdi Baba's presence speaks of more than formal Islam, just as Sathya Sai's outer integration which appears emphatically Hindu, conceals the fact that his being far exceeds conventional Hinduism—or any other ism.

11

Daily Round, Common Task

For someone confined to an urban existence, even a day's excursion to Puttaparthi from Bangalore will prove to be a tonic. Nature is encountered at her own pace, creaking bullock carts replacing fume-spewing diesel transport. The healthy graces of a calm and fresh natural order restore the inner rhythm as the bus delivers you to the ashram gate. Prasanthi Nilayam sits alongside the village of Puttaparthi, occupying higher ground āway from the river.

Anyone who has made a prolonged stay in Puttaparthi learns just how essentially backward it remains. Even a few years ago, one had to go to all the way to Bangalore to get items like a steel nail (which can hold a photograph of Sai on a cement wall) or a small spanner (for unscrewing the top of a tap). The village streets, though perked up behind modern cement facades cheerfully tricked out in bright colours, remain primitive when it comes to discovering items of comfort or convenience. Poverty and backwardness remain the lot of most, though many villagers are now on the threshold of a cash income undreamt of by their parents. They have sold their plots to developers at a premium and the profile of the main village street has been transformed from a line of tottering stalls into high-rise luxury apartments.

The two economic levels that are found within and outside the ashram are not overtly hostile to one another, thanks to the reconciling presence of Sathya Sai. If he had been an outsider settled here, there would have been an undeclared war between locals and the ashramites (as at Pondicherry and Pune for example). Because this local boy has brought honour and benefits to his village, he is adored as much by his poor neighbours as by those of richer means who come from afar for his blessings. This explains why Sathya Sai, preaching for two generations in a Naxalite-infested area and travelling regularly between Puttaparthi and Bangalore, a distance of some 150 kilometres by (till recently) poor roads, has never been troubled by outlaws. In fact, Sathya Sai's social concerns are manifest in the many vocational training centres he has opened to alleviate the chronic rural unemployment. It is a characteristic of Sai Baba that even in the whirl of some VIP visit he will find time to hand over a gift to the dignitary's driver. These small acts are noted by the poor and they are not taken in by stories that Baba only cultivates the rich. Though the large Purnachandra and Sai Kulwant halls were donated by rich industrialists, they enable the ordinary villager to join in the ashram activities protected from the elements.

Although Baba's institutions are now spread over several kilometres, the old centre remains untouched and his living quarters are but a stone's throw from the Ganesh gate. For many years, Ganesh was the only deity installed on the Prasanthi campus but recently shrines to Subramanium and Gayatri have been built. These must be the only shrines in the whole of India that have been designed to *prevent* offerings being made. Outside the ashram campus cynics point out that one reason for the surge in consecrating temples to the Sai saints is that the financial returns are both handsome and immediate. You hear claims that even in a small mofussil town, public donations to the tune of fifty thousand rupees a day are collected. Rather than weaken the argument for the upsurge of genuine mass feelings, these statistics strengthen it since the offerings are not solicited but freely and enthusiastically made by a cross section of the community. The images of Sai Baba have caught the public imagination and human affection in matters of devotion is one of the few constants that defy the world of changing fashions.

Around Baba's plain residence, barrack-type blocks of flats for the devotees were constructed in the 1970s whose pink and blue livery cheer up these early utilitarian buildings. Later blocks built for better-off followers have been better planned with trees and gardens interspersed. These flats (leased out by Baba to chosen devotees), which have now made Prasanthi a township, distinguish Puttaparthi from Shirdi. Because of the presence of their living teacher, devotees make longer stays in Puttaparthi. Each small flat has a kitchen and bathroom space behind the main living-cum-sleeping room, which is fronted with a veranda to cater to the overspill of devotees at festival time. Puttaparthi is as austere and businesslike in its lifestyle as Sathya Sai.

When the ashram rules first appeared in print in 1962, the ashram day started at 4 a.m. and finished at

10 p.m. (Nowadays lights-out is at 9 p.m.) They advise 'everyone should speak soft and sweet' and caution against making any kind of offering 'except prema' (love). So popular had Sathya Sai become in the south that a year later *Sanathan Sarathi* was forced to carry Baba's warning against tricksters cashing in on his name to collect funds: 'Some rogues have gone to the extent of printing letterheads in Baba's name and sending letters as if written by him asking bhaktas to part with money to the persons named in the letter, namely themselves.' For many, the discovery of their spiritual dimension through some sudden and unexpected contact with Sathya Sai comes with little understanding of the reality of the psychic realm. Innocent of worlds other than the waking one, these newcomers to the feet of the Puttaparthi master are fair game for the clever rogues who stalk in the shadow of Sathya Sai and claim to have been given special powers by him. Incredibly, even the most hard-headed of businessmen, because of the unfamiliarity of the spiritual milieu they find themselves in, can fall prey to the smooth ministrations of these conmen. The bazaar outside the ashram has grown into a regular hippie destination, with carpet sellers from Kashmir, ear cleaners from Uttar Pradesh and German bakers from Manali. The sleaze that has spread from Goa's beaches has a toehold in Puttaparthi because many of the foreign disciples are both rich and foolish, and make for targets no tourist tout can resist. It is hard for new adherents to accept the ground rule of the Sai Parampara's protestant ethic: no priest, tout or middleman comes between the teacher and his pupil. There is direct contact on several planes and, unless specifically stated, the instructions transmitted are

strictly for the private consumption of the devotee. Puttaparthi has its share of disciples who, from a sense of self-importance, spread items of information that were confided for the growth of their souls only. In the study of any life of the Deccan masters, it is vital to check whether the information revealed stems from an objective authority or from an enthusiast with an agenda.

A day in the life of the ashram begins for the visitor at 5 a.m. with the chanting of the *aum* in the so-called temple. However, not everyone is given the liberty to join in. The charged early-morning atmosphere is made more eerie by intent volunteers who, like school prefects, supervise the lines and pounce on any articulator of the sacred syllables (repeated twenty-one times) whose voice does not match up to the high music of the occasion. These old devotees, who maintain the strict standards of ashram practice, will have arisen much earlier and, having performed bodily ablutions and household puja, stalk the cool air of the plateau to offer obeisance to Ganesh before taking up their duties at the prayer hall. For their master Sathya Sai, the day has begun considerably earlier. Like Shirdi Baba before him, sleep seems to be a low priority and resting of the body seems to be a better description of how the night hours are passed.

After the *aum* recital comes the south Indian rite of *suprabhatam*, the melodious awakening of the gods. This is followed by chanting of the Vedas to purify the locale. As an extension of these rites, devotees gather to march around the ashram campus for *nagarsankirtan*, the singing of bhajans to induce thoughts of God in the empty streets and bless those who will walk through them. Nagarsankirtan usually accompanies the dawn chorus of

Prasanthi's prodigious bird population who flap away from their Sai sanctuary to feed in the surrounding fields. The ear of the devotee is thus led from the inner reverberations of the *aum*, muffled by the temple walls, to the public expression of hymns sung both by humans and birds. Nagarsankirtan is led by a band of brahmins chanting auspicious Sanskrit shlokas and represents a nod in the direction of orthodoxy. However, this is the only acknowledgement of the presiding grace of the twice-born. For the rest of the day the ashram follows its logo, honouring the message of all religions and recognizing in Sathya Sai not a sectarian priest but God made visible in human form.

Inspired by morning darshan which takes place around 6.30 the devotee is charged to perform 'seva' (good works) for the betterment of the world. To the visitor, darshan appears to be a tedious wait that puts strain on both mind and body, forced as one is into the unaccustomed posture of watchfulness. Under these trying circumstances—where an hour or more may pass, sitting on a stone floor uncomfortably, while awaiting the arrival of Sathya Sai—it seems that the philosophers have got it wrong about freedom being humanity's defining instinct. Fidgeting seems a much more likely candidate. To add to the mounting irritation of too much mental and too little bodily activity, is the behaviour of one's neighbours who subtly shift by slow degrees in seeking to gain a better view by crowding out those in front. Bonhomie demands that strictures are implied rather than voiced, but occasionally a person who has waited long hours to assure his place in the front row explodes in vexation when someone at the very last moment seeks to plonk himself down right in front, blocking the view.

Twenty years ago, darshan was bestowed in the same area which was open to the heavens. Before the mandir was given a facelift and the soothing sandy surface replaced by unforgiving stone slabs, there were palm trees against whose boles one could rest one's back. A spacious relaxed air pervaded the proceedings and the devotee was free to carry his bag with books, camera and, most importantly for urban bottoms, a well-padded cushion. Otherwise the routine was much the same as it is today. If you wanted a good seat you had to join the darshan queues early. Baba was more accessible in the sense that no college campus had yet been started and he would be the sole figure who patrolled the veranda. It could get very hot or very wet, and those few odd-ball devotees who insisted on sitting it out in these extremes would be rewarded with Baba's personal darshan, though not in the way they would have hoped. Signalling towards them from the veranda upstairs, Baba would tap his head to indicate they were mad and should make themselves scarce. This was done in such an affectionate manner that no censure was implied. They knew he was only concerned for their physical well-being.

The Sai Kulwant darshan hall, over the years, has increased in extent and opulence, and appeals greatly to the simple villager as a sign of *virya* and *aishvariya*—the splendour and inexhaustible wealth associated with an avatar. To old devotees, the swaying palms were preferable to today's ornate moulded ceiling bedecked with a glistening array of chandeliers. This extraordinary enclosure can seat up to 40,000 devotees. Alongside stands the Purnachandra auditorium for cultural shows which seats 10,000 comfortably. Regional religious festivals are celebrated in these public areas and at Dussehra, Vedic rituals are performed with meticulous regard for ancient practice.

It seems strange that gathered for darshan are (in the off-peak season) more than 10,000 people, all with their eyes riveted on the appearance of a small, slight figure who now appears as a flame-like apparition as he glides silkily along a red carpet. Everyone, according to his perception of divinity, will have his instincts confirmed. To a few he is but an insignificant, frizzy-haired villager dressed as a holy man, disappointing in stature and capable it seems only of producing a handful of miraculous dust. To others he comes with clouds of glory betokening a cosmic energy greater than a thousand suns, the saviour of the three worlds and the man born to rule the kingdom of the human heart. Now that physical disability has forced his arrival by vehicle and curtailed his movements, making his stay much shorter, it is noticeable that the crowd, which formerly waited on after darshan for completion of bhajan, will immediately disperse when Baba's car withdraws, in brusque demonstration of their preference for personal aura over religious rite.

Over the years the impact of Sathya Sai's darshan begins to have a lasting effect. The process echoes the alchemical art of transmuting base metal into gold. Most old devotees have learned to regard Sathya Sai's ability to transform them from ordinary mortals to something infinitely more meaningful as the greatest miracle. And it is through repeated darshan that this miracle slowly unfolds. Those who are indifferent to Sai's aura of grace shut themselves out from its benefits while the seekers of his blessings, in opening themselves to what he has come to give, are rewarded bountifully. For some, the most satisfying thing about darshan is witnessing the physical reality of a local boy who, by dint of self-imposed discipline, confidently walks amongst his fellow villagers and is accepted by them as a role model of their ideals. God and the supernatural are secondary to local pride in having fathered forth from Rayalseema—one of the poorest areas in the whole of India—this wonder of the spirit.

Between the hour of darshan and the singing of group bhajan, the eager will line up to seek a place in the temple prayer hall where arati will be performed, not to the gods, but to the guru as the climax to the singing. Although Sathya Sai, like Shirdi Baba, gracefully accepts the validity of the feelings expressed by the devotees, he moves away quickly to signify that it is not his outer form that is being worshipped. Similarly, Sai Baba will make a token gesture of occupation of the ceremonial throne, only to indicate that his body represents the divine unseen guest.

After these ceremonies some devotees may look for a seat closer to the darshan area where Sathya Sai may walk later in the day. However, for most normal appetites—sharpened by the wonderful plateau air—the various canteens both inside the ashram and outside call for breakfast. After this light repast, devotees do household chores including the Puttaparthi drill of buttonholing the dhobi. The wearing of plain, clean white clothes that mark the campus uniform can only be maintained by efficient laundry arrangements. The size and smoothness of the clothes-washing operation at Puttaparthi is astonishing and is performed in the traditional manner of pounding the garments against stones set up along the (usually dried-up) course of the Chitravati. One of the many less-regarded miracles of the place is how these illiterate dhobis keep track of some hundred thousand items per day, each with its identifying mark to distinguish it from thousands of similar lookalikes. For the dhobi, Sathya Sai's insistence on modest clean attire has been a godsend. To assist these mammoth washings, Baba has built proper dhobi ghats and dug deep to provide groundwater to service them.

To some, the milling sea of laundered white kurta-pyjama or bush-shirt and 'pant' (the favoured costume for Baba's college students where the sleeves are worn long and the pants are of cotton drill) exudes the aura of a spiritual bourgeoisie since in India no peasant can ever dream of wearing laundered clothes except on special occasions. Those who can afford to wear such luxuries (and change them twice daily) are not in the least self-conscious since India's cultural norms are being honoured and these loose-fitting clothes are ideal, both for Puttaparthi's climate and for sitting on the ground. The moment these ashram visitors leave its compound, they will revert to the 'suit-boot' of the educated city dweller. Puttaparthi to them is a kind of vacation for the soul where traditional Indian values are invoked to satisfy both the inner and outer man. Politics, cricket and television are for once studiously left at home, though the morning newspaper can be found outside the ashram gate.

The canteens at Puttaparthi are another miracle in their smooth ordering. The secret behind their success— tasty food provided cheaply—is Sathya Sai's personal interest in the daily fare and his insistence on sampling the menu before bestowing his blessings. In the characteristic south Indian fashion, the main canteen is run on efficient lines with sparkling stainless steel utensils laid out on marble-slabbed tables, where a dozen devotees can sit in line, each on his fixed stool. Volunteers both prepare and serve the food, and it is given in generous helpings since most village appetites, when it comes to the shifting of rice, are voracious. Coupons for the meal's components are bought at a booth outside and this allows the diner to vary his choice of dishes. Thousands of devotees are fed swiftly and hygienically in this south Indian canteen. For those unaccustomed to a diet of rice, other arrangements are available.

The north Indian canteen provides chapattis, vegetables and dal favoured by the Punjabi palate. Here, the clientele is smaller and the atmosphere less hectic. Also there is the novelty of a buffet presentation so this canteen makes for a pleasant change after the staple south Indian rice–sambar–rasam routine. A third canteen caters to western non-spicy tastes and, though expensive, provides good nutritious food even if it seems driven by the latest diet fads. Outside the ashram are innumerable small cafés and restaurants that cater to the casual visitor who is not overly concerned by the ashram's advice to stick to the officially sponsored canteens where Sai Baba's grace comes as a bonus with the food.

For those backsliders who find vegetarian food a slight on their digestive rights, some local enquiries will soon bring them to a shack where meat is discreetly consumed. Despite the pressure to disapprove of these minority tastes, the fact remains that the poor of the surrounding villages eat what they can get. The ashram's spiritual concern to educate villagers is laced with an understanding of these everyday realities. After all, Sathya Sai was brought up in these surroundings and knows exactly what goes on. For his own food, Sathya Sai prefers local vegetarian fare but the intake is so negligible as to be worrisome. He is said to be fond of ragi (finger millet) balls, which traditionally has been a rich source of energy. Small helpings of local vegetables and perhaps some pickles form the rest of the meal, which may be followed by a regional sweet and (formerly) paan. Loyal cooks, attuned to his likes, have the honour at times of accompanying him on his tours and even the ladies who grind his favourite chutney may find a place in his entourage. Though rather small in quantity, the cooking for Sathya Sai involves the strictest security. Only the very old and trusted devotees are charged with this duty, echoing the courtly traditions of the Deccan, where the king's food-taster was a highly regarded position. There are several well-attested instances of attempts to poison Sathya Sai and his immunity is interpreted by some followers as evidence of his Neelkanth status (the name of Shiva referring to his ability to neutralize the effects of poison).

Unlike in so many ashrams, at Prasanthi food and drink are not viewed as a grim necessity. Sathya Sai takes joy in providing such amenities and when the fashion of ice-cream parlours hit India in the 1980s, Puttaparthi's campus soon followed Bangalore and Hyderabad in opening an outlet. A whole line of shops was added for devotees and students, placed near the centre of the ashram and adjacent to Baba's quarters where he could

oversee the pleasure of his disciples. Some years later, for
security reasons, a more distant shopping centre was built
where, after evening darshan, devotees can gather for ice
cream or coffee. The atmosphere here is subdued, markedly
different from the cafés outside where some devotees are
tempted to mix their spiritual search with worldly profit.
It was presumably to keep them away from such
temptations that Sai Baba encourages his own devotees to
run stalls that provide most of the visitors' needs.

In the noontime heat the ashram wears a somnolent
air. For visitors there may be time for a siesta before the
queues start forming at 2 p.m. for evening darshan at
four, but for residents and volunteers their daily grind
allows no respite from duty. Prasanthi runs with a
minimum of supervision and maximum of conscientious
service. To sit idle is to offend the raison d'etre of being
there: learning how to serve one's fellowmen better. Jobs
are not apportioned as much as entered into from a spirit
of wanting to be useful. Since Sai Baba is a perfectionist,
the hours are long and the rewards in outward recognition
negligible. Like in most ashrams the residents are forced
to work on themselves and, because of the huge numbers,
their contact with the guru they serve grows more restricted
by the year. Those who view Prasanthi as a haven for the
idle rich to escape from the real world and follow a
private spiritual fantasy have not cared to examine the
views of the inmates. The longer they stay the more
difficult their lot becomes because Sathya Sai, sure of
their loyalty, now turns his attentions to a new batch of
entrants and appears to the oldies even more distant in
his bestowal of favours.

The evening darshan of Sathya Sai will appear to be

the climax of the ashram routine by virtue of the crowds it draws. Visitors pour in by bus and (of late) by train, and all the college and school students belonging to the Sai institutions join in to swell the attendance. Foreign devotees often come in groups (distinguished by a coloured neckerchief) and a good many of them are non-resident Indians. Sathya Sai's appeal is not just spiritual but extends to the fields of culture, education, medicine and even psychology. Practitioners of all these disciplines find in him a refreshing guide, free of academic cobwebs and unencumbered by the blind belief that Western science can provide all the answers.

Darshan is a colourful congregation, made more inviting by the openness of its appeal. The curious, dedicated, hopeful, thankful, angry, depressed, handicapped, fulfilled, disturbed, desperate—all conditions of humanity in fact—foregather in expectancy, searching for an answer to why life has treated them the way it has. No one wants to end up like Emperor Aurangzeb who on his death bed confessed, 'I came alone and do not know who I am.' For the past forty years some have witnessed this drama of the human soul rising up to ask questions of itself (in the form of this slight, orange-clad figure) on a daily basis. Never does the thrill of a Sathya Sai darshan pall nor its tangible glow fail to hearten. It is a moment of rare love, equivalent to feeling briefly like the richest person in the universe.

Like everyone else, I have never failed to be uplifted by the mere sight of this stand-in for the divine. There is this baffling stream of energy between him and his disciples that works its magic on the audience. What one sees is not just a transfigured son of the soil but the

potential of divine grace realized in human form. Here is
the climax to my search for witnessing grace in action.
Extraordinarily, it descends again and again, year after
year, as if Sai Baba is taunting the critics who demand a
sufficient volume of statistical proof.

No one outside his peasant admirers will see just
Sathya Sai in the dress of a holy man; all recognize the
miracle of an incandescent soul which has made universal
a provincial body, achieving in one lifetime the grace
conventional religion teaches us is the work of several.

*

Given the Indian milieu, the way Prasanthi runs itself is
extraordinary. The crowds maintain silence, observe the
rules restricting their display of devotion and generally
cooperate with the ashram authorities to allow Sathya Sai
to devote all his energy to his mission. From the beginning,
the democratic mood has been characteristic of Sai's
mission and during the early days in the Old Mandir, he
was available at all hours to attend to the needs of the
disciples. It was from the ranks of these devotees that the
organization of the volunteers grew into a Seva Dal. The
ashram interfaces easily with the township of Puttaparthi
and to know how much the latter depends on the
physical presence of its most famous son, you must
witness its deserted status when Sathya Sai is away in
Whitefield, his second ashram on the outskirts of
Bangalore.

A large measure of the peaceful atmosphere at
Prasanthi is due to the steady and unobtrusive labours of
the Seva Dal volunteers from each state (and abroad)

who oversee crowd control and the day-to-day running of the ashram. They bear what Baba has called 'the burden of the badge' and, as distinguishing badges, the men wear a blue neckerchief and the ladies yellow. 'You will earn my grace more by service and sacrifice than by sitting in the front line and nodding to whatever I say,' asserts Baba and this is hard to live by when they have travelled so far only to gaze at him. Out of the thousands of genuine workers there will be one who breaks the rules and surreptitiously allows a poor relation in to sell photographs of Baba on the sly. Back in their home states, these foot soldiers of the Sai mission hold weekly meetings in their localities where social and educational work is performed on a voluntary basis. This network of Sai branches now extends round the world and Sathya Sai is the spiritual equivalent of the United Nations in the number of states where he has followers. Unlike other churches, none of his followers from 150 nations have been born into his movement. All have joined in response to the love he embodies.

On occasion, Baba would voice his displeasure at the devotees just as Shirdi Baba used to do. In such a tight-knit society where horizons are consciously limited to intensify the work on oneself, the only outlet is for gossip, factionalism and the urge to demonize those who irritate. Earlier, Sathya Sai would perform inspection tours of the campus and would not hesitate to give a tongue-lashing to old resident disciples, a grace most of us would rather forego. He would accuse them of singing bhajans so badly that it made him want to put cotton wool in his ears. He would chide the old disciples for their petty politicking and sending him telltale letters full of jealousy against newcomers. He complained about the dirt and rubbish outside their rooms, so characteristic of orthodox India's one-pointed concern for spirituality. They would let their room maintenance run down and then expect Baba to repair and paint it. Sometimes he threatened to send the scandal-mongers away and (like Gurdjieff) close the ashram except for a handful of sincere workers. Baba would dramatize how much he was doing for his disciples and how ungrateful they were in not changing their ways. How bad they must be, he would remind them, when they forced even an avatar to use hard words.

It has to be added that having delivered himself of this diatribe, Baba would revert to his compassionate self within minutes. In those days, before the crowds came he would intermingle with the disciples, visiting the sheds to check on living conditions, and joke with everyone he passed. I remember then how Baba would love to have his photograph taken and would pose for anyone who had a camera. Nowadays, for security reasons, cameras are strictly forbidden. In fact, even pens are not allowed in the darshan area and a uniformed police officer has been attached to Baba's entourage.

12

For Mine Eyes Have Seen

Due to his long, steady and unchanging ministry, Sathya Sai has seen three generations of devotees who have offered their full-time services. Many of the young guru's early devotees have passed on. Second-generation disciples are still in residence and each, in his or her small way, owns a niche in Baba's heart for their faithful companionship. Professor Kasturi is widely known for his literary efforts but what is not known is that Sai Baba, as with all his close disciples, put him under a lot of pressure to perform. Living in Prasanthi Nilayam is real sadhana where to lose one's cool for just a moment can set the seeker back months in the quest for elusive equanimity. Some have compared life in Prasanthi to being inside a pressure cooker.

The number of disciples who deserve mention for their loyalty is legion and they come from all backgrounds. For example, Shivraj Patil, currently India's home minister, is a devotee, as was Dr Bhagavantam one of the nation's leading scientists. For many years Bhagavantam translated Sai Baba's public speeches from Telugu into English.

Royals, diplomats, politicians, artists, musicians, singers, dancers, designers, sportsmen and film stars, all can be seen in the Puttaparthi darshan lines. To get an idea of the range of fine minds that have been attracted to Sathya Sai's message, the reader is referred to the various commemorative volumes that have been published to celebrate Baba's more significant birthdays. For example, *Golden Age* (1980) includes a brilliant article on the meaning of religion by Krishna Iyer (the judge who attempted to include the whole of Hinduism in one definition) and an equally inspired overview of the same subject by the distinguished administrator, K. Guru Dutt.

An early close disciple was Raja Reddy, for many years the lead singer at bhajans whose devoted attendance on Baba seemed to make him his right-hand man. Everyone assumed he would be a permanent fixture but, as always with Sathya Sai's mission of love, nothing is predictable. Raja Reddy's marriage, arranged by Baba, was the talk of the ashram. It led to a life outside Puttaparthi. (The arranged marriage of disciples has become a regular sign of Baba's grace. However the casualty rate, as in any activity involving the clash of egos, can be high and this has led some to conclude that Baba's powers are imperfect. To make an arranged union work is the responsibility of the partners involved.)

Colonel Joga Rao is another character in his own right and one of the very few whom Sathya Sai could relate to as a friend. Baba loves to banter with his close disciples but those of a traditional upbringing consciously create a gap between what they consider divinity and their own unredeemed state. Joga Rao, being of a life-affirming disposition, was a breath of fresh air in situations where sanctimonious attitudes could be mistaken for spiritual. It is worth mentioning here that Baba's sense of humour and fun-loving nature puts any study in English at a disadvantage in that it is not possible to capture either the earthy flavour of Telugu or Baba in his natural element. He always pokes fun at the elderly devotees' romantic inclinations and some of these jokes border on the bawdy. Once, after Dussehra, he remarked that the best way to clear the lingering crowds would be to put Kasturi on stage with Shirdi Ma (an equally ancient disciple). Seeing them dance together the crowd was guaranteed to melt! Whenever he greeted the latter he would affect surprise and say, 'What! Still not dead?' At Diana Baskin's wedding, Baba, with his usual humour, said to another lady devotee, 'I have a good husband for you—120 years old.' His humour is essentially of the rural variety and, like Shirdi Baba's, direct, unaffected and original. He addresses most devotees as *bangaru*, meaning 'gold', and the well-fed are referred to as 'pakoras'. He often uses the phrase '*ayyo papam*' which could be interpreted as an affectionate greeting to an 'old sinner'. It has been true of both the Deccan masters that they have never occupied the high ground of morality. They are well aware of their visitors' shortcomings and broach their weaknesses with a fine sense of delicacy. Though not always. I recall in Delhi, Baba asking the son of a wealthy businessman who had come to meet him wearing a pair of tartan golfing trousers, '*Kya carpet pehen rakha*? (Are you wearing a carpet)'

Kutum Rao, the ashram administrator for several years, was another close devotee who brought his experience as a high court judge to bear on its orderly running. Two volunteers, Patel and thereafter Khayal Das, with their wrestler's physique, were employed to shadow Baba during his darshan rounds those days and dissuade overenthusiastic devotees from ambushing him. Another familiar presence, still seen on the temple veranda waiting to ring the arati bell and wearing the only white Gandhi cap in the entire assembly, is none other than the nephew of Manohar's keeper. From looking after Shirdi Baba's dog, this family now bears Sathya Sai's ceremonial silver mace.

An Andhra disciple who makes no bones about his world-affirming preferences is Ramana Rao, a bluff Seva Dal organizer. His book *Love is My Form* (2000), written straight from the heart, is refreshing in its approach. It reveals Sai Baba as a warmly humane elder brother rather than a distant pious figure. The directness of Raman Rao's love is revealed in the very first remark by a friend who took him to see Sai Baba against his wishes. The friend's guarantee was, 'I will show you God.' Baba invariably addresses Ramana Rao as 'Rowdy' and it is extraordinary to read how he seems to have set snares to catch this prize devotee, aware that under the chief executive's façade lay a heart of gold. The author gives a brief but telling description of how, on his first visit to Puttaparthi, he met a famous early disciple Surayya (Suryaprakasha Rao) who ran the canteen in an authoritarian style, and whose towering height had caused Sai Baba to nickname him 'Coconut Tree'. According to the author, 'his voice was a cure for constipation'. Surayya had been an employee of the raja of Venkatagiri, who, of all the early disciples, was the most dynamic. The raja worked unceasingly to further Baba's cause and was instrumental in widening his popular base. Everybody loved the raja since his devotion was both sincere and flamboyant. Baba was a regular visitor to the small former state of Venkatagiri and between these two there was a beautiful relationship in the classic Indian mould where the wisdom of the guru guided the energy of the king.

A lady disciple who brooked no nonsense was Rani-ma's mother, Kanwarani Balbir Kaur, a sardarni from Patiala. The sequence of events that led to her joining the ashram is an oft-repeated story. Sai Baba intervened directly to save her life. In spite of her precarious health— the best doctors had in fact given up on her—this lady supervised all the lady volunteers, no mean task considering that the locals regarded her as an outsider from the north. Sai Baba understood that the Kanwarani was what the Sikhs call a 'sawa-lakh' character, worth a whole army in her fighting spirit. Having beaten death by cancer on the operating table, she arrived in Puttaparthi to take on the formidable challenge of shaping the landscape for the upcoming Prasanthi Nilayam.

Another formidable lady disciple from the north is Brij Rattan Lal who sacrificed Bombay high-society life to bring her family business expertise to Sathya Sai's printing project in Whitefield. It is thanks to the Rattan Lals that *Sanathan Sarathi* became the vehicle of enlightenment, spreading the word of Sathya Sai to the four corners of the world.

In what is probably the most remarkable account of life in close proximity to Sathya Sai, Diana Baskin's book *Divine Memories of Sri Sathya Sai Baba* (1990) describes two years of literally living as Baba's next-door neighbour in Whitefield. Like the bizarre decision to have a young American couple live next to him, this book is so full of surprises that it completely inverts the image of Baba as a reclusive touch-me-not figure. These recollections show him as a caring, affectionate neighbour, full of fun and laughter, far removed from the austere, religious personage depicted by some devotees. Diana was a great animal lover and Baba once performed a miracle that saved a dog's life, a small act of mercy done consciously out of love for a disciple's soft heart.

It will not be out of place here (in view of Diana's love of animals) to make mention of some of Sathya Sai's four-footed devotees. The largest and most enduring is Baba's elephant Sai Gita who came as a calf and seems to behave like an affectionate daughter on ceremonial occasions. Among the more unusual ashram inmates were some camels donated by a devotee. Over the years, many dogs have left their mark, the most famous being two Pomeranians called Jack and Jill who were reputed to fast on Thursdays. Jack slept at Baba's head and Jill at his feet. When they passed on, Baba raised a small memorial over their remains to mark their faithfulness. (Shirdi Baba had a pet horse as well as his dog, while Ramana Maharishi had a dog he used to send round the foot of the holy mountain to act as a guide for pilgrims.) Besides being fond of small breeds, Baba has also kept Alsatians. A wonderful canine study showing them straining at the leash is captioned 'Baba with Tommy and Henry'. This happens to echo a pose often adopted by the mystic guru Dattatreya. As noted elsewhere, Puttaparthi boasts the most remarkable bird life with countless thousands coming home to roost in the trees scattered over the campus.

It seems that Sai Baba had recognized the makings of a true disciple in Diana, and her book about her search for inner reality is testimony to the courage and honesty perhaps only a woman can rise to. Everything about this woman's devotion seems genuine. Although belonging to Hollywood high society she had connections with the Krishnamurti foundation. She was married (unhappily) to Joel, another Hollywood type who was as casual about the inner quest as Diana was serious. Strangely, Baba took a liking to Joel and to everyone's astonishment invited the couple to move in alongside his Whitefield residence. Though marred by marital quarrels and bickering—told with rare honesty—their time spent with Baba makes for fascinating reading. The reader is provided a marvellous close-up of Baba's parental affection for his adopted foreign family. From the outset, humour characterizes the relationship, such as when Baba presented Diana with a medallion that shows him unflatteringly with his front tooth missing! Before he met Baba, Joel would refer to him as 'that character' and say that he would not be convinced of Baba's credentials unless he produced something really big, like a rainbow. The day they reached the ashram they were astonished to see a rainbow that instead of curving went straight up into the heavens. When they met Baba, the first thing he asked Joel was, 'Well, character, how you did like the rainbow?'

It seems Joel's crass American view of life was a novelty Baba wished to sample, but when his relationship with Diana did not improve, Baba recommended they end it. As it happened, Joel, despite his wife's advice, underwent an operation and died. Since the couple had a growing daughter, Baba insisted Diana remarry and said

he would find her a suitable partner. The new husband
was an American lawyer younger than Diana but as both
were Baba's disciples they agreed to do his bidding, albeit
with the westerner's shock at the lack of any romantic
overtones. Both were bemused at Baba's insistence that
they produce a son forthwith. When the couple duly
complied and returned to India with their baby for Baba's
blessings, he chose to cut them dead. For four long years
Baba refused to acknowledge their presence. This severe
test of loyalty was something Gurdjieff specialized in.
Few can survive the guru's switch from affection to
supreme disdain. Some turn bitter and write books
denouncing their master; a few like Diana and her
husband stand fast and find the guru's love in one
another and pass the icy ordeal.

Baskin's story of the sudden freeze after the warmth
of Baba's neighbourliness makes her book an absolutely
authentic description of the actual treading of the inner
path with its hazards and pitfalls. It shows how
unpredictable this form of Shiva (the inner guru) can be
and how risky it is to portray him as either a traditionalist
or a modernist. Diana's discerning eye notes how the
delicately feminine clings to the strongly masculine in
him, echoing the Shiva–Shakti union. She also notes how
his complexion can change from ivory to dark brown. In
short, he is unique, one of a kind. She quotes an unusual
saying that brings home how original Baba's views can
be: 'To aim at a lion and miss is better than hitting a
jackal.'

The most objective account of Sai Baba's life and
leelas in English is by Howard Murphet (*Sai Baba: Man
of Miracles*, 1971). Murphet, a no-nonsense Tasmanian

with a terrier-like instinct, approaches Sai Baba's miraculous aura with all his critical faculties working. Perhaps recognizing that here is one Boswell genuinely alive to life's miraculous nature and keen, from altruistic motives, to share it with others, Sathya Sai responds positively and demonstrates a remarkable range of seemingly divine powers before this one-man scrutinizer. Murphet comes across as a sound seeker, reliable witness and impartial reporter, though it is true that by the end of his findings he is turned into a confirmed believer.

Along with a theosophical background that has enabled him to appraise the authenticity or otherwise of psychic phenomena, he brings the rare gift of writing about spiritual matters in normal everyday language. His diaries of days spent in physical proximity to the Puttaparthi saint, at a time when the Sai movement was still manageable in numbers, are also useful for their social content since they list the people from the top end of society who sought out the saint's aura. What is noticeable is the continuous turnover of devotees. It is as though Baba urgently wants to get as many people started on the path as he can. They come, are bowled over by Baba's love and attention, come again and are hooked. Thereafter, Baba welcomes new faces and the old begin to feel neglected. Some fall off, others find Baba within themselves.

After the phenomenal and well-deserved reception of his first book on Sathya Sai, in 1978 Murphet published an account of his second visit to India. It has the same impressive mix of respect and restraint in seeking to gauge the status of a person who appears to have no equal in the extraordinary feeling of the numinous he gives off. If the first book on Baba's miracles appeals to the man in the street, the second, *Sai Baba Avatar*, addresses the queries of more specialized students who want to understand Sathya Sai's baffling qualities. Those with a scientific bent of mind demand statistics, preferably from the pen of a doctor of philosophy. Realizing that this is a prerequisite for Sai Baba's attributes to be taken seriously by a doubting world, Murphet marshals the evidence convincingly. It appears that Sathya Sai, since his earliest childhood, has produced vibhuti and other small objects at the average rate of roughly twenty-five manifestations per day. This means that to date more than half a million so-called miraculous demonstrations of this minor kind have been effected in public by him, adding up to an overwhelming body of evidence.

To back these facts scientifically, Murphet quotes from the report of two academic researchers, Dr Otis and Dr Haraldsson of the American Society for Psychical Research, who performed fourteen experiments in the presence of Sathya Sai and concluded that what they had witnessed bore no evidence of fraud and was unknown to science. To show the rigorousness of their research, they note that it would be easier to fake the materializing of dry substances (like vibhuti) but admit that Baba could also produce wet and greasy items. Both researchers were excited by their findings and the prospect of their changing the face of science. At the same time they were realistic enough to know that modern science is but another form of priestcraft that guards its dogma jealously. During the Middle Ages in Europe, theology was known as the queen of sciences and the modern world was announced by dislodging the pre-eminence of theology. Science now has the respect of the masses and the heady power that attaches to such belief. It is hardly likely to willingly abdicate its power in favour of such an unquantifiable reality as love. Science, especially medical science, some would argue has become the world's most fashionably expensive superstition.

Murphet's third book, *Sai Baba: Invitation to Glory* (1982) goes into further study of psychic phenomena and starts with the author's personal treatment at the hands of a famous Philippines psychic healer. Murphet's is a sane voice and keeps the subject firmly in the realm of the possible. Because he is a bird of passage he slips up in recording some minor cultural details, but the transparency of his motives and the generosity of his spirit in seeking to understand Asian customs makes his writing a worthy exposition of the Sathya Sai message. Mixed with deliberations on how the phenomena works are examples of dramatic healings witnessed by the author and all this is told with a sense of compassionate involvement that gives the book its value.

Prompted by Sai Baba, Murphet reluctantly produced a fourth, largely autobiographical volume that makes for a moving testament to the genuine quest of self-discovery of an ordinary mortal. *Where the Road Ends* describes his early life in Australia where he trained to be a journalist and how fate landed him in England just as the Second World War was declared. Overcoming his pacifist principles, he joined the army and rose to the rank of colonel, his journalistic background ensuring that he was not exposed to the gore of the front line. However, this did not prevent him from having to face the horrors of Belsen and from witnessing the ensuing Nuremberg trials.

Murphet recounts his lifelong interest in exploring any spiritual movement that came his way and the sincerity of his search was rewarded by his profound feeling of having arrived after his darshan of Sathya Sai. The guru in turn seems immediately to have recognized in Murphet a sound vehicle for spreading his message abroad.

His fifth book, *The Light of Home* (2002), is dedicated to Shiva and is a mellow summing up of a rewarding life-pilgrimage. The author maintains his buoyancy of spirit and the humaneness that characterizes his writing to the end. Thanks to Murphet's inbred modesty, readers can identify with him as a trusted guide. Unlike the usual prose in praise of Sai Baba there are no gushing tributes or exaggerated claims. The success of all the five books by Murphet lies in their low-key presentation of a modern master whose extraordinary aura can—with his grace—be experienced by the most ordinary of seekers. The unaffected style of the Australian author guarantees that the subject of spirituality is investigated with the objectivity demanded by any science.

One of Sai Baba's closest foreign disciples is Dr John Hislop, an American whom he would put in charge of supervising the running of the Sai mission in the USA. Like Howard Murphet, Dr Hislop is a dedicated note-taker and has published two collections of his conversations and correspondence with Sathya Sai. Unlike Murphet, who tests Baba's credentials before accepting him as his guru, Hislop fell under Baba's spell straightaway. He talks of how his parched, soulless, intellectual self immediately found water when he met Sai. Hislop was serious about his search. It was on a Monday that he heard of Sai Baba's ability to actually change a person's character. By Thursday he was on a plane to India. This also indicates he was a person of means but Hislop's saving grace is his indifference to wealth and an innocence which is unusual in a businessman.

Baba, in turn, immediately took a strong liking to Hislop and granted him interviews on a regular basis. Unlike Murphet, who comes across as somewhat clinical, Hislop's conversations are those of a surrendered disciple at the feet of his master. The style of his writing is akin to that of Kasturi's, full of devotion expressed in adulatory tones with little trace of the critical faculty at work. Sai Baba responds enthusiastically to this willing suspension of disbelief and showers his time on this shining example of surrender, a large-hearted man genuinely working on his ego to reduce its size. Hislop has the humility to stand back and distinguish between his physical and immortal self. He is acutely aware of his limitations but, instead of bewailing them, he instead celebrates Sathya Sai's limitless state. The reader feels that these two in conversation are akin to Arjuna being taught by Krishna.

Hislop's winning innocence is reflected in his earlier search for a teacher. Like many others, he was what my guru called a 'stamp collector', doing the rounds at various ashrams, looking for the teacher who would be right for him. Like Murphet, there is a tenuous Theosophical connection. He begins his search on the California campus of Krishnamurti, the promised avatar who preferred to stay human. After a stint with the world-weary Krishnamurti, he found Maharishi Mahesh in whom he perhaps saw his own innocence reflected. Practising transcendental meditation (TM), Hislop soon achieved the status of an initiator. The Maharishi then invited him to India to locate land for an ashram in Uttarkashi.

Both Murphet and Hislop passed through the TM phase and it is interesting to compare their reasons for feeling they had outgrown it. Murphet owns no regrets and adopts a gentlemanly tone of farewell, commending the Maharishi's efforts to awaken our modern material age to its spiritual heritage, and acknowledging the help he had received from the movement. Hislop, when performing the prescribed period of intense meditation, broke through to a promised level of bliss. However, his refined soul immediately recognized this as not a genuine spiritual state but a phoney substitute. Realizing that he would be responsible for initiating people into a pseudo-spiritual experience, Hislop chose to resign.

These departures from the TM fold are in stark contrast to the Beatles whose disenchantment at the Maharishi's methods is recorded in Nancy Cooke de Herrera's *Beyond Gurus* (1992). According to this socialite's eye-witness account, they walked out of the Maharishi's Rishikesh ashram in a state of shock, feeling betrayed at the businesslike wheeling and dealing they found there. (By contrast, when some of the Beatles visited Sathya Sai and found they were treated in his ashram just the same as any other devotee, they did not stay.) Lest Nancy Cooke's whirlwind tour of Indian spirituality be written off as just another tourist's impressions, her book reveals a person of considerable intrepidity and understanding. Her description of what she felt when confronted by Sathya Sai at a Puttaparthi darshan is the most honest I have come across. Women react more instinctively than men in such matters and the full wonder of love is hinted at in her extra-feminine appraisal: she feels a wave of exultation wash over her again and again like an orgasm—only better, as she puts it. She notes that it never happened with the Maharishi.

Hislop's books *Conversations with Bhagavan Sri Sathya Sai Baba* (1978) and *My Baba and I* (1985) reveal a rapport based on genuine brotherliness and, in the presence of such a reliable disciple, the guru can relax and lapse into a lighter vein. The conversations are of a nature shared by friends and deal with practical matters of ashram administration, especially the handling of money and how to deal with awkward disciples. For the first time in a biography of the Sai Parampara, the ease and warmth of the interchange shift the emphasis from the glory of fulfilled divinity in the guru to its real possibility shining through in ordinary disciples like Hislop. One of Baba's students neatly sums up this breakthrough when he calls Hislop 'a small portion of Swami'. Too often the Puttaparthi master is portrayed in the aloof unattainable mode and there seems to be no urgency amongst the disciples to strive and emulate his glory. The very fact that Sathya Sai was born aware of his divine status is discouraging to many and gives others an excuse to argue that no ordinary mortal can hope to achieve such an advanced state. Hislop's steady trickle of love is a great worker of miracles and proves that any devotee who strives to become one with the ocean can discover hidden reserves within. At a Sai-sponsored international symposium held in Rome in 1983, Sathya Sai's message concluded, 'What is the use of all this knowledge if man does not know himself? Man's inner reality cannot be

188 Sri Sathya Sai Baba

known by exploring the world outside.' He accuses
science of limiting our individuality to that of a wave
breaking on the shore. Quite the opposite is the case,
insists Baba: beating in the heart of each one of us is the
ocean.

Amongst the few really perspicacious books in English
about the Sai phenomenon, Dr V.K. Gokak's *Bhagavan
Sri Sathya Sai Baba: The Man and the Avatar*—written to
commemorate the fiftieth birthday of Sathya Sai in 1975—
is the most lucid. Gokak was an academic of all-India
standing as well as a Kannada litterateur of distinction. It
is interesting to note that his forenames 'Vinayak Krishna'
encompass the gods of both Shaivite and Vaishnav
traditions. Significant because Sathya Sai, though appearing
to be essentially Hindu, never displays any preference for
either the Vaishnav or Shaivite sects by which most
Hindus identify their religion. Moreover, Gokak was a
poet and translator with a masterly command of English.
Of all the biographers, Gokak is the most learned and
best qualified to supply the background details of what
avatarhood entails. Sai Baba would treat him as a friend
and, like Hislop, Gokak's naturally modest soul never
sought to abuse this privilege. If anything, Gokak was
more submissive than the American since the awesome
implications of avatarhood are apt to be lost on non-
Hindus. As a seasoned academic, Gokak would go straight
to the heart of any philosophy and point out its strengths
and weaknesses. As a humanist himself, he saw through
the posturing of some rationalists and charged them with
ignoring realities like the soul and love because these
categories are difficult to quantify. To Gokak, life was
poetry, and Sai Baba seemed to him to be Shiva come to
open the third eye of love.

When an American devotee-turned-critic published a book (Tal Brooke's *Lord of the Air*) in an attempt to smear Sai Baba's reputation and call him the anti-Christ, Dr Gokak took up the gauntlet to set the record straight. His *In Defence of Jesus Christ and Other Avatars* exposes the doctrine of hate that inspires and funds such books. It has been a common pattern over the years for overenthusiastic westerners to jump in the deep end of Indian ashram life and then blame India for attempting to drown them! (At least the Beatles, when they left the ashram of Maharishi Mahesh in a huff, had the grace to admit that they had expected too much of him. Listed among their disappointments was his failure to halt the ageing process.) One of the alarming aspects of the inner path is that it tends to attract the unstable character and my own guru admitted that the first thing he had to guard against when taking on a new disciple was incipient madness. Not even a guru can heal a sick mind. Certain rival missions feel threatened by Sai Baba's popularity and are envious of the exponential spread of his message. Once favourite disciples whose egos are deflated by being relegated to the back row can become prime targets for these missions, ready to fan any smouldering resentment into fire.

In recounting this sampling from a multitude of Sai devotees, it is pertinent to mention that a high proportion of devotees started out as doubters. Sathya Sai approves of this cautious approach since finding a genuine teacher is like walking through a minefield. Howard Murphet recalls how his very first contact with Baba was preceded by his interrogation of a British theosophist who had just returned from Puttaparthi. Murphet eagerly asked this

visitor about the genuineness of Sai Baba and the reply
was couched in characteristic British understatement: 'If
Sai Baba is a fake,' averred the theosophist, 'I'll go back
to beer.'

{13}

Filling the Hungry with Good Things

The most visible miracle at Puttaparthi, after the grace of Sathya Sai's physical presence, is the single-handed achievement of Sai Baba the builder. In the astonishing array of public works that light up this once benighted area, he seems to have been both inspired by the bouldered beauty of the Deccan landscape and provoked to outmatch it. One of the extraordinary features of the backward Rayalseema region is how the local people have always thought big architecturally. Hampi, even in ruin, is more impressive than most modern cities of India. Today, Puttaparthi gives further evidence of this Andhra talent to raise memorable buildings. Few Indians would place Andhra on the map of architectural impressiveness yet ruined sites like the Kakatiya capital at Warangal and the Buddhist stupa at Amravati (amongst others) astonish by their scale and finesse. Only forty kilometres south-west of Puttaparthi is the fabulous temple of Lepakshi, a superb structure endowed with awe-inspiring works of art both for their size and aesthetic impact. The innermost chamber of the temple has a huge fiery mural in honour of the Shaivite deities of the Lingayat order and outside the temple is the serene monolith of the deity's vehicle, Nandi. This superb giant sculpture of the bull, done on site from the pink granite boulders that litter the landscape, is said to have been crafted as a labour of love in the masons' spare time. It is the biggest Nandi in the subcontinent. (Curiously, this ancient and characteristic image conveying the Deccan's devotion for Shiva is absent from the Puttaparthi campus.)

Puttaparthi's impressive spread of architecture reflects this imaginative ability to not only think big but build impressively. Significantly, Sathya Sai's approach differs from that of the emperor Krishnadeva Raya who erected several huge freestanding gopurams in the south to declare his power. At Puttaparthi, the lone gopuram is only thirty feet high, signifying that here architecture, like religion, is designed for the common man. The massive enclosure of Sai Kulwant Hall, skilfully grafted on to the temple building, is familiar to all visitors. More deserving in terms of architectural merit, but less visited because of its hilltop site, are the pleasing lines of the university administrative building. To some, the colour scheme of pink and blue that is common in the Puttaparthi campus seems to argue for the popular taste of the ordinary Indian and this is exactly its target audience. Sai Baba's residence and the other structures are made to resemble the villagers' romantic notion of heavenly pavilions.

*

All practitioners of true religion show concern for the physical welfare of mankind. Unlike conventional religion which promises the underfed their fill in the next life, true religion demands that health care and nutrition be provided here and now. All the world's compassionate teachers have been agents of healing, personally intervening to heal the sick and make whole the bodies of the suffering. The Buddha, like Shirdi Baba after him, would take on the diseases of others. Gurdjieff and Sathya Sai are remarkable for their unorthodox doctoring of patients, performing seemingly magical cures and, in the case of Sathya Sai, even resorting to surgery. It is significant that both teachers affirm the world and celebrate life in the present. They believe in action now to counter the dormant pull of tired religious attitudes which accept suffering with a fatalistic shrug and put it down to past karma, to be dealt with by destiny in the hereafter.

Christ's healing miracles indicate the path of true religion which matches uplifting sermons on the mount with down-to-earth medical treatment. To Sathya Sai, his whole mission is to provide health care to his immediate neighbours since highfaluting ideas about the divine have no meaning to ailing and underfed bodies. India's most cherished spiritual doctrine of Advaita, which sees the soul in everything, tends to ignore the harsh fact that such edifying insights can only arise in someone with a full belly who doesn't have to worry about where the next meal is coming from.

Modern India's health care is a badly ignored area where poor hospital facilities are swamped by a sea of acutely suffering patients. At the same time, chemist shops dispensing medicines rake in huge profits (sometimes stooping to the sale of spurious drugs) while students fight to win places in medical colleges for the rich pickings that await them when they qualify as doctors. Like medieval priests who sheared their parish flocks, some modern medical professionals wax rich on the sufferings of their fellow men.

It is to try and provide an alternative direction to stem this rot that Sathya Sai has set up his hospitals, colleges and water projects. Without these basics the noble doctrine of religion is a non-starter. The crying need is to demonstrate to an acquisitive society that the satisfaction people think possession of money will give them actually stems from service to humanity. This attitude of compassionate seva has been inculcated in the devotees at Puttaparthi from the earliest days. This it seems is the real reason why the divine chose such an unprepossessing place as Puttaparthi to furnish an agent for furthering its mission. Mankind's understanding of religion has become too cerebral and self-serving and the grim statistics of post-independence India show that the gap between the rich and the poor is widening. As a laboratory of the world's religions where experiments in understanding the divine have always been part of its culture, modern India has, in Sai Baba, a rare exemplar who would make it his mission to demonstrate the inherent divinity in humanity.

*

Medicine in India does not come cheap and many families bankrupt themselves in seeking relief for their family members through expensive medical treatment. It was to answer this need that the Puttaparthi super-specialty hospital was raised, demonstrating to the poor that their concerns were foremost in Sai Baba's thoughts. Opened on his birthday in 1991, the Sri Sai Institute of Higher Medical Sciences specialized in cardiology, uro-nephrology and ophthalmology. A postgraduate institute was also set up. Subsequent developments led to modifications in the hospital's field of reference. Built next to the airport on the approach to Puttaparthi, this sprawling campus, was, as is the norm, approved and supervised by Baba in every detail and came up in the phenomenally short span of eight months.

Baba's latest super-specialty hospital—another ambitious project designed to bring to the poorest the best medical care in the world—opened in 2001 at Whitefield. The hospital was built in record time on land donated by the Karnataka government. Here is a clear demonstration of 'Sai sankalpa' (will power) being actualized by 'vajra sankalpa' (lightning remedial action), rather unusual in the Indian milieu of chronic procrastination. Amazingly, Baba had the inspiration to build this hospital one morning and by the same evening, the site had been viewed and earmarked. The hospital has an eco-friendly design and provides free diagnostic, medical, pre-operative, surgical and post-operative services. It boasts state-of-the-art medical care in cardiology, cardiac surgery, neurology and neurosurgery, and there are plans to provide postgraduate training. Baba has designed a spacious temple of healing where the grand but soothing architecture alone is a tonic to the patient.

India has an average of only three hospital berths for every thousand of her citizens and the hospital at Whitefield provides 333 beds. The very latest procedures are followed here and the modern air-conditioned setting almost embarrasses patients accustomed to the rough-and-ready treatment meted out at village dispensaries. Patients who are poor are given precedence and among them, young mothers, children and breadwinners are treated on a priority basis. All treatment is free. Because of the subcontinent's excessively high rate of heart disease (more than a million children suffer from heart ailments in the country) there is a special emphasis on cardiac care. In the first six months of the hospital's opening, some 1,300 operations were performed in the twelve operating theatres. Patients from all over India and Bangladesh are treated irrespective of their religion. Sadly, for every child treated, hundreds have to wait their turn.

Involved with the problem of medical care is the problem of aftercare. Many malnourished patients who come from long distances on a doctor's recommendation (which is mandatory) are operated upon successfully. They then return home where their poverty does not allow the post-operative regimen to be followed. Many die from dietary deficiency and this means that operations costing several lakhs of rupees go waste. Despite their often futile outcomes, these operations are testimony to Baba's generous impulses and they do generate a morale-boosting effect on the poor who know that at least someone cares for their crushing condition. Another dismal reality among the poor is that some are driven to the desperate extreme of selling a kidney to raise cash. For this reason, certain operations are not carried out in Baba's hospitals to avoid any distressing fallout on the healthy. The medical philosophy behind Baba's health-care programme is to provide holistic treatment to the patient's body and spirit, creating a de-commercialized atmosphere where the value put on human life is not cheapened by the urge to make money out of anyone's illness.

Needless to say, Baba's charitable policy is a very expensive proposition. This is where the Sai Central Trust, created by Baba and manned by handpicked devotees, comes into the picture. Till recently it was chaired by Indulal Shah, a chartered accountant from Bombay with a long commitment to Gandhian ideology. Baba is the chief trustee and only he is empowered to sign cheques. This arrangement means that Sathya Sai, in effect, owns nothing personally. This in turn frees him from the common charge faced by many modern godmen of not keeping their ashram accounts in a transparent manner.

Thanks to Sathya Sai's gifted managerial instincts, his critics cannot find fault in the ashram accounting nor, for that matter, snare him into materializing undeclared gold. According to official statistics, Sri Sathya Sai's mission has been the largest recipient of foreign donations in recent years. (Unlike many gurus, Sathya Sai does not solicit donations nor has he built any temple where monetary offerings are made. Too often in India the money that finds its way to the hundi box is tainted from the exploitation of the poor, and rich businessmen repair to these temples in the hope that the deity's forgiveness can—like most things—be bought.) These donations are deployed in running institutions where expenses, as in the case of modern super-specialty hospitals, can go up to a crore of rupees per day. This is because not only do the salaries of highly qualified surgeons have to be paid but also the total cost of the latest operating techniques has to be borne, since all treatment is free. This has been Baba's cardinal principle in starting these state-of-the-art hospitals. The poor must avail of the latest advances in medicine and cannot be expected to pay for it.

*

Chronologically, after the village hospital set up to fulfil his mother's wishes, Sathya Sai turned to education. The Anantapur College for women marked a breakthrough, challenging the barrier of orthodoxy that has kept India bound despite her declared freedom. Although proud of India's ancient values, Sathya Sai, rather than be disheartened by the nation's lacklustre performance since Independence, took on the task of showing what could be done when love, instead of self-interest, became the tool for development.

In the field of education, human values are stressed and emphasis is placed on drawing on culture and tradition to strengthen a student's spiritual identity. Sathya Sai's educational system aims to cut the knot by providing a fresh perspective to students. Known as EHV—education in human values—the system emphasizes character building and giving the student self-confidence. The Indian student is provided proper exposure to Indian culture. 'The end of education is character,' declares Baba, 'and the end of knowledge is love.' The continuity of love's informing spirit is indicated in the line of impressive school buildings which announces the township limits of Puttaparthi. Each caters to a different age group and has distinguished frontages immaculately maintained amidst well-tended greenery.

When the first modest start was made in institutional education, Baba's car passed some boys trudging back to their village in the midday heat after attending the inaugural ceremony. Immediately, he got out and, sitting by the roadside, ordered his driver to use his car to ferry the boys to their homes. Several devotees' cars were also pressed into service and since there were 300 students Baba had to sit for three hours until all were delivered.

In contrast to most well-run schools in India which copy the British system of education, the students at the Sai Vidya Giri (hill of knowledge) follow the Indian style of dress, wearing plain white cotton clothes but of modern cut. The Sri Sathya Sai Institute of Higher Learning, founded in 1991, is a deemed university and offers arts, science and professional subjects both at the undergraduate and postgraduate level. Its administrative building, crowning the hilltop above the Prasanthi campus, is a powerful symbol of the blending of the religious and secular, and must rank amongst the most handsome structures in the township. Sai Baba is also concerned to keep the poor people abreast of the latest educational tools and he constructed a Space Theatre (planetarium) to encourage them to marvel not just at astrology but astronomy. The newest building, Chaitanya Jyoti, which houses a museum, synthesizes Gothic arches, Moorish domes and a Chinese sweeping roof, pointing to the oneness of the spirit that has brought to Puttaparthi visitors from all over the world.

As with all of Baba's conferred blessings, at no point in his education is the student made to pay for his schooling. At the same time, the beneficiaries are taught to cherish the gift of helpfulness and pass on to others what they have received. Besides a sound academic instruction, the student is given a firm grounding in civic responsibility and taught the value of service as the greatest contribution he can make to society. The students are actively involved in village development programmes where they are able to see at first-hand the region's woeful backwardness. In the long run, revitalizing of the gram sabha (village council) will be Sathya Sai's greatest gift to Rayalseema.

Professor Gokak has described the educational philosophy and the method of teaching of the Sai educational programme in *Bhagavan Sri Sathya Sai Baba: The Man and the Avatar* (1975). He begins by giving Baba's own forthright views on the shortcomings of modern education. Baba likens modern graduates to degree hunters who have turned what the goddess of learning has to offer into an undignified scramble for jobs. He deplores the fact that nowhere does modern education introduce the student to 'the joy of enquiry into one's own reality'. He also regrets the fact that many schools treat their students as numbers rather than names. Humaneness is the only basis on which student–teacher trust can be founded.

Baba's remedy is the re-establishment of the four pillars of truth, duty, peace and love, on which can be built the four-fold path of self-confidence, self-satisfaction, self-sacrifice and self-realization. The National Assessment and Accreditation Council has recently accorded the Sri Sathya Sai Institute of Higher Learning its topmost grade and considers it a 'crest jewel in the university education system in the country'. According to Dr Gokak, who once had to nurse a sore head when stoned by the students of Bangalore University, these reforms could not be implemented a day too soon. But to show how the academic world is at odds with itself, another vice chancellor turned out to be Sathya Sai's most vociferous critic. Dr Narasimhaiah arrogantly insisted that Baba should 'submit' to questioning about his 'so-called' divine powers. Ironically, Dr Narasimhaiah shared similar views with Sai Baba about making education more accessible to the poor. Gokak's last words on the direction education in India should take are worth repeating: 'Our national system should be rooted in spirit in accordance with the genius of the country. It aspires to train the individual in the process of self-sculpture.'

*

After providing education and medical aid to the surrounding population of Rayalseema, Sai Baba was faced with the region's other perennial problem: shortage of drinking water. Not only is water basic to the life of the villager, it is the secret of his good health. There is a fairy-tale touch to the story of Baba's miracle in addressing the water crisis in the region. As a boy farmed out to work for a cruel sister-in-law in Tamil Nadu, the young Sathyanarayan Raju daily lugged pots of water from the Krishna canal on his back. Baba still bears on his body the weals caused by carrying these pots as a child. The boy never complained and, in fact, rejoiced in doing a chore that Shirdi Baba had taken upon himself. It was no doubt the excruciating drudgery of this task that prompted Sathya Sai to undertake his revolutionary drinking water scheme for drought-prone Rayalseema. He knows better than anyone the blessings of piped drinking water.

Because Rayalseema falls between the path of both the southwest and northeast monsoons, it has been chronically short of water throughout history. The tank at Bukkapatnam was a medieval attempt to store this precious resource. P. Sainath's acclaimed *Everybody Loves a Good Drought* (1996) is a thought-provoking study on well-intentioned government schemes that dispense funds to drought-prone areas. As the book shows, most of the funds intended for the relief of small, distressed farming families never get past the district administration officialdom. The money is swallowed up by petty officials in league with rich contractors. The author notes that Anantapur, the rustic district headquarters some fifty kilometres from Puttaparthi, is, going by the sale of luxury four-wheel vehicles, ranked as one of the richest towns in India. This is thanks to drought-relief money that gets diverted to the car showrooms via corrupt officers and conniving contractors. Another appalling—and connected—statistic for Sathya Sai's home district is that, in the three years preceding the millennium, nearly 2,000 poor farmers took their own lives after crop failure from drought. Unable to repay their loans on fertilizers and pesticides they committed suicide by swallowing the latter.

Faced by this morass of moral decay and suffering on his doorstep, Sathya Sai set about the Herculean task of solving the problem of drought his own way. What the government could not achieve in fifty years he accomplished in three. The Sri Sathya Sai Water Supply Project, executed at a cost of 300 crore rupees now supplies 700 Rayalseema villages. Where finding potable water once involved a long walk daily by womenfolk, now there is a tap in their own village with a constant, clean supply. The project consists of four schemes. The first involves comprehensive gathering of water through infiltration and collection wells along the Chitravati, Pennar and Hagari seasonal rivers. The second entails direct pumping from a balancing reservoir above Anantapur and treatment through rapid sand-filtration. The third comprises seven summer storage tanks that tap—when available—water from the Tungabhadra canal. The fourth, covering nearly 300 villages, involves drilling deep bore-wells, construction of storage tanks and the laying of pipelines.

In 1997, on a motorbike traverse of the Deccan from Shirdi to Puttaparthi, I was riding through some wild upland country between Uravakonda and Anantapur. As I crossed the watershed ridge, I stopped at the Pennahobilam temple oasis perched on the crest. There was something magical about this site and, as I descended into a dell to discover its secret, I came upon a small spring of clear water purling out of the peninsular granite slabs, a singularly unexpected bonus on this climb through bleak heathland. The heart's ease I felt there, I would later realize, was due to the fact that this was the source of the Sai Water Supply Project.

This lifeline, like all the other projects of Sathya Sai, was accomplished in a phenomenally short period. Two thousand kilometres of pipelines were laid, twenty balancing reservoirs were constructed on hilltops, nearly 300 overhead reservoirs were raised, and over a hundred ground-level reservoirs built. Some 1,500 precast concrete cisterns, each with four taps, were provided for villagers.

Incredibly, most of the pipe laying was completed within three months. Even more incredibly, on completion of this project, Sathya Sai set about executing another to the north of Anantapur in Medak and Mahboobnagar districts which guaranteed water to another one million Andhra villagers. This brought the total of villages covered to 1,100. To cap this performance of selfless service, paid for by the devotion of Baba's world following, the entire project was donated to the government of Andhra Pradesh.

This is not the end of the story. In 2002, Sathya Sai sanctioned his trust money to complete the Telugu Ganga canal, a narrow water course that had been started by the governments of Andhra and Tamil Nadu a generation earlier (to help ease Madras's acute drinking water shortage) and had been completed—at least on paper—in 1996. Because of apathy and corruption however, no water ever reached the thirsty citizens of Madras. Baba commissioned the 176-km stretch between Kandaleru and Poondi to be strengthened and lined with concrete, contributing thereby three lakh acres of irrigated land to Andhra. Eighteen months after declaring his intent, Sathya Sai made the Telugu Ganga flow. Fittingly, in view of Sathya Sai's mythological connection with Shiva and his own unique ability to wave a magic wand over any project he touches, the canal now goes by the name of Sai Ganga.

The whole atmosphere in Puttaparthi is alive with Sathya Sai's prime concern to look after his devotees' needs. When I have stayed in the ashram, the room rates have been extremely reasonable and a small daily rent is levied to cover water and electricity charges. Those who stay in the sheds, as I did on my first visit, are not charged. The meals in the ashram are heavily subsidized as is the devotional literature on sale in the Sai bookshop. Most of Baba's devotees are poor and many come long distances at considerable expense if they travel with their families. It is this family feeling existing between Sai and his following that makes Puttaparthi a vibrant and meaningful experience. The family extends to the bird life and an extraordinary feature of the ashram campus is to be deafened by the sheer volume of birdsong as crows, mynahs and egrets come each evening to roost in the trees surrounding Sai Baba's quarters. If you phone Prasanthi as dusk settles, the noise of the birds is so great that it drowns out the voice of the person called. There is an uncanny connection here with the magnetic pull Sathya Sai has on his human followers. It is almost as if we have an avian Pied Piper in residence who offers sanctuary to his huge and appreciative—if raucous—choir.

Sathya Sai, who reposes a passionate faith in India's future, has a devastatingly simple technique for breaking societal apathy to development projects: appeal to a human being's finer nature, see the divine in every face, demonstrate love, and work for the common good. Even the hardest of hearts will melt before this appeal. Baba has come to heal and the work goes on through him, not by him. 'When your faith meets my love, there is cure' is a profound holistic truth that has been echoed by all religions. It is the nature of life to be compassionate, Baba argues, and therefore no power can ultimately triumph over that divine mandate. We do not now recall the enemies of Christ, the Buddha and Mahatma Gandhi, and history will not record the names of Sai Baba's critics. Mankind does not honour those who carp but those who deliver. A study of Sai Baba's phenomenal contribution to the physical and mental health of his Rayalseema constituency reveals the hidden hand of the divine. This, it seems to the student of religion, is the only explanation for the explosion of compassion in such a short span of time, causing Prasanthi Nilayam to emerge from a bare plateau, drawing to it as if by some magnetic property, people of all creeds from all over the world who come voluntarily, pulled by the urgency of love's beckoning and not by any promises of pie in the sky.

Lessons above Contemplation

To the world at large, the Sai Baba phenomenon is associated with the public display of miracles. Given that Sathya Sai's own brothers and sister were initially reluctant to accept his miraculous nature, it is hardly surprising that the rest of the world is chary of pronouncing on its genuineness. Traditionally, Indian masters have cautioned against the display of psychic powers since they can distract the seeker from moving to the higher spiritual level. It seems that in harnessing the miraculous to further its message, the Sai Parampara is making another statement of its independent and unorthodox credentials. Today, when, after centuries of being associated with snake charmers and yogic rope tricks, India seeks to assert itself as a modern nation, any mention of supernormal behaviour raises the hackles of rationalists who dismiss all such claims as superstitious nonsense designed to fool the unlettered citizen. While there is everything to be said for the proper policing of frauds who misuse religion and its psychic component for personal gain, there is something perverse in refusing to accept the obvious. What is assumed to be motivated by the scientific temper may just be intellectual snobbery that involves the obduracy of ingrained bias.

The problem with a miracle is that it does not allow for easy objective verification, though we know it to be true. From the outset we note bias, negativity and self-importance in the so-called scientific attitude to miracles. Miracles threaten the foundations of their cult of reason and have to be demolished or explained away at any cost. Also to be considered is the mindset of the viewer. Those with an imaginative bent see more miracles than the mind scrupulously attached to the scientific method. But scrupulous attachment is not the same as detached objectivity and scientists can be as stubbornly superstitious about their discipline.

Caught between these extremes of science and inspiration, the common man exercises his prerogative of applying common sense to what is claimed as a miracle. For millennia, the peasant sowing seeds on the bosom of mother earth to feed his family has been aware of the inherent grace of her response. Nature's cycle is a constantly recurring miracle on which our lives depend. Another obvious miracle all of us, rich or poor, experience every moment of our lives is the beating of our heart. Where on earth will you find a pump that comes with a seventy-year guarantee and requires no change of oil or mechanical overhaul—provided you treat it with a healthy lifestyle? Everything about the human heart is miraculous. People monitor the development of the human foetus all the time yet fail to register its miraculous origins right before their eyes. One moment (in the womb's embryo) it is not there, the next it is. Eastern wisdom holds that in the bliss of bodily union, when the twin egos are transcended by their oneness, the soul descends into its chosen situation. Thus, while at the physical level the parents imagine the child is of their choosing, in the spiritual sense the child actually has chosen its parents. (Compare Sathya Sai's remark, 'Children come through you, not to you.')

By seeing the human heart as a physical pump we underestimate its divine potential. It is our passport to the realm of lasting things, rarely used and forever subordinated to the decisions of the mind. Unlike a mind, no matter how well schooled, the heart (because of its divine roots) is not host to illusions. The greatest illusion is to ignore the heart's miraculous powers which alone can make sense of the mind's churnings. Complementary to the classical belief that the mind must be stilled before it can know God, Bhakti teaches that the heart should be activated.

Presumably, those who are deaf to the miracle of their own heart's beating are bound to be blind to the aura that Sathya Sai gives off. Such minds are more concerned with spotting deception in the materialization of vibhuti and reducing it to the level of a magician's trick, despite half a million public demonstrations of this siddhi. To compare Sathya Sai to a professional entertainer is not just an insult to someone immune to insults, but a belittlement of our inmost being. To doubt the promptings of your own heart is to be afflicted with a disease worse than death.

According to the senior jurist M.N. Krishnamani (*Divine Incarnation*, 2001), a case was filed in the Andhra High Court accusing Sai Baba of contravening

the Gold Control Act as he materialized gold lockets for
his devotees. The pettiness of this complaint was exposed
when the court pointed out that the act forbade the
manufacturing of gold, not its creation. How tragic that,
though born with a heart full of wonders, some men can
be so insensitive to the reality of their own being and,
despite repeated demonstrations of spiritual wonder, keep
parroting the charge of legerdemain.

According to the philosopher Locke, 'A miracle I take
to be is a sensible operation which being above the
comprehension of the spectator and in his opinion contrary
to the established course of nature is taken by him to be
divine.' A miracle—like a disaster—is an act of God that
our waking mind refuses to make provision for. For most
miracles appear to offend the natural laws. But to those
few convinced that nature, and the life force that manifests
through it, are themselves miraculous, such expressions
of wonder seem to be the proper appurtenances of the
human soul.

Miracles are what Sathya Sai calls the visiting card of
the divine, indicating that he is a conduit, an agent of
that power. We all are to some extent, as the following
small incident will show. I was standing on the roof of
the palace at Jaisalmer, writing some notes in my diary,
when the swirling wind dislodged a picture tucked between
its pages. The day before I had been to Nathdwara and
had bought a picture of Srinathji, the distinctive black
Krishna of this pilgrim place. The picture was caught in
an updraught but instead of being blown away it spiralled
slowly down to land at the feet of a woman who entered
the palace gate precisely at that moment. She picked up
this visible sign of grace and hugged herself with joy,
thinking only of the blessings of Krishna rather than

work out where the picture had come from. This arguably was a miracle since it would be impossible to replicate the behaviour of the wind, the paper and the woman. But the point to be noted is that the woman felt it to be a miracle.

Science makes no allowance for the reality of psychic phenomena and will conclude, for want of physical explanation, the psychic and spiritual levels attained by great souls throughout history are fallacious. Science makes fun for example of the claim of 'virgin birth' that is common to many religions. Not just Christ and Krishna but also Merlin and Plato enjoy this status. To turn it into an article of blind belief seems just as unimaginative as ruling it out as impossible. When asked by a pundit whether he was begotten or created, Sathya Sai referred the questioner to his mother Easwaramma for a reply. She spoke of a 'big ball of blue light that glided into' her. Married at the age of fourteen, she was now entering her eighth pregnancy, having lost half her progeny, according to village lore, to the black arts. It is against these crude realities governing village India, where pinched economic circumstances are worsened by gross superstition and mindless custom, that Sathya Sai's coming seems so miraculous. In Puttaparthi's backward and primitive milieu, he appears an oddity as though set apart from his brothers and sister, and spiritually on an entirely different plane. Immaculacy here refers to the undeniable fact that the grace that has come into the world with Sathya Sai is unique in being deathless. Hence that which does not die cannot be born. All those who astonish the world with their seemingly immortal gifts tend to acquire similar status through mythology.

*

His boyhood leelas tend to obscure the spiritual challenge
Sathya Sai had to overcome in asserting his real nature.
His boyhood and subsequent career is strewn with
miraculous happenings that all his biographers attribute
to his inherent divine nature. They choose to ignore the
fact that even the small act of producing vibhuti is a
psychic drain because sacred ash or any other materialized
substance does not appear effortlessly of its own accord,
but is willed by psychic energy.

A story is told of the school-going Sathyanarayan
who came across a British officer out on a shikar trip.
The car had broken down and the driver appealed to the
locals for help. Sathyanarayan lectured the sahib on the
evils of taking life and, his having finished the lesson, the
car miraculously started. Needless to say, Sathya's father
was appalled at the possible fallout of his precocious son
holding back the car of a British official and haranguing
him in the bargain. It is amusing to note how Kasturi has
updated this story to make it seem eco-friendly, with the
boy-guru advising the sahib to shoot only with a camera
and donate any orphaned wildlife to a zoo. Whatever the
accuracy of the details, it shows how courageous and
devoted to the cause of compassion this young student
was.

This kind of mechanical miracle is popular amongst
villagers who have little knowledge of technology. An
oft-quoted 'miracle' is how a holy man offloaded from a
train for travelling without a ticket displayed his yogic
powers and prevented the engine from restarting. The
holy man went on to make a career based on this incident
and the superstitious public named him after the railway
station where he had been detrained. The psychology that

occasioned this supposed miracle (the likes of which, incidentally, have decreased dramatically with the introduction of diesel/electric traction) was that the steam-engine driver panicked on hearing his family cursed by the yogi. As a result, he opened the regulator too much, causing the engine's driving wheels to spin instead of gain motion. The genuine teacher has no need of such contrived situations that play on human fear and ignorance. Sathya Sai's extraordinary nature has been arrived at by constant application, a physical sadhana that astounds by its unrelenting commitment.

Against this light of the spirit that characterizes Puttaparthi, the reality of black magic in the outlying villages is a grim reality few are willing to acknowledge. With a higher literacy rate than the north, the villagers of south India ought in theory to be less addicted to the seamier side of religion. But in practice, their access to knowledge has led to an adeptness in the use of magic. Just as Professor Kasturi skirts the ground realities on the prevalence of witchcraft in favour of mythological euphoria, so does orthodox Hinduism conceal the fact that most of the Vedas are concerned with the rituals of magic rather than the philosophy of the spirit.

Sathya Sai's mission, from the beginning, was to wean away the villagers from the primitive superstitions of popular Hinduism to the more respectable Greater Vehicle, where the local blood-lusting demons are replaced by the yogic majesty of a compassionate Shiva. His first battle therefore was the harshest since he had to take on the crude majority with its vested interest in maintaining the old order. The boy's brahminically inspired instincts, until they became public knowledge, worked against him and reveal how multilayered is the mansion of Hinduism. The confrontation with his father saw the victory of the Greater Vehicle. (To the popular mythologizer of course, Puttaparthi was in no need of liberation since in phantasmagorical ages long ago it was peopled with enlightened beings who predicted its golden age to come under Sathya Sai.)

It was necessary for the young teacher to hold his increasing daily audience by constantly referring to orthodox brahminical teachings. Only when his authority was established could he reveal the full message of the Sai Parampara: namely that all religions are one. For the rest of his long ministry, Sathya Sai would have to balance the need to hold his village following, with their attachment to the Puranic scriptures, along with his universal appeal to an international audience.

The problem with the young master's miracles was not just that they offended the reason of the intelligent, but that they occured so often that they tended to devalue the awe that traditionally surrounds divinity. Hundreds of thousands of people have witnessed the production of vibhuti from close quarters and it hardly seems like a miracle now. To answer those critics who feel true miracles should produce objects larger than the human fist can encompass, on two separate occasions, during the Shivaratri festival, I have seen Sathya Sai produce phenomenal amounts of vibhuti from a small upturned wooden pot held over a large silver tray. Seated on the tray in his foot-clutching posture was a silver image of Shirdi Baba. With sleeves rolled up, to the accompaniment of bhajans sung by a frenzied audience, Sathya Sai's arm worked with such animated physical energy—scooping out clouds of billowing vibhuti first with one hand then with the other—that Kasturi, who was holding the pot, had to hang on grimly to avoid being swept off his feet. This vigorous scouring of an empty pot, resulting in a mounting heap of vibhuti that covered the entire image of Shirdi Baba, went on for several minutes before Sathya Sai reeled away exhausted. He was back again within a short period, as usual, with his powers apparently replenished.

What is as miraculous as the cascade of vibhuti is the fact that for the few seconds it takes Baba to remove one arm from the pot and insert the other, the vibhuti stops falling. The moment he reinserts his arm in the pot, the ash pours out in billowing abundance. This astonishing evidence of large-scale materialization, performed annually for many years in front of huge congregations (along with its sequel of Baba bringing forth the lingam from his person), can be viewed on film at the Chaitanya Jyoti museum. To the devotee, this is the sure sign of Shiva's blessed presence. To the scientist, it is beyond his normal comprehension. For an objective witnessing student of religion, the verdict has to go in favour of genuineness. The arch-rationalist, Vice Chancellor Dr Narasimhaiah, was particularly concerned about the small size of Baba's materializations and this reveals just how unscientific such investigators' concerns are. What has size got to do with whether a thing is real or unreal? Negating what we see repeatedly just because it is small and we do not have a name for it is highly unscientific. The claim that public entertainers and illusionists can repeat the materializing of Shivaratri vibhuti is implausible. What prevents them from demonstrating their claim?

The lengths to which some critics will go in their claims to disprove the authenticity of such phenomena prove absurd. A film taken by the BBC claims to show Sai Baba surreptitiously passing a necklace concealed under some books he was presenting to a distinguished visitor. In fact the film sequence—which can be slowed down for closer inspection—shows nothing of the sort. What it shows is what every observer for the past seventy years has seen for themselves; one moment there is nothing, the next an object (in this case a necklace) has appeared as though hurled from psychic space.

*

There are different categories of miracles. There are those objective oddities of nature which are affected by magnetism. In Ladakh, on the road to Leh for example, an empty vehicle will move uphill of its own accord with the engine switched off apparently due to some sort of magnetic attraction. From purely physical phenomena we move to the second category—psycho-physical happenings. A good example would be the impossible feats of strength performed by my father when he was sleepwalking, which I personally witnessed. My father who suffered from a bad back could, when he was asleep and in the mode of sleepwalking, move heavy furniture single-handedly. Once as a boy I watched him move a piano which three men put back in place with difficulty the next day! Murphet and Hislop have described similar phenomena in their books on Sathya Sai. Unlike the Indian devotee who is emotionally fulfilled at the sight of a lingam being brought up from Sathya Sai's stomach, the western mind wants to work out the mechanical process involved. Intriguingly, Hislop suggests that the lingam Baba gives birth to follows nature's pattern and its molten state solidifies like lava from a volcano in the throat. When I witness Rani-ma's lingam (produced by Baba's grace), its solid metal feel reminds me of how the rocks on our planet have been formed from molten magma. What has taken nature aeons of time to transform appears through Sai Baba to happen in a trice.

Murphet has described the even more remarkable and unlikelier instance of a chunk of granite being turned into sugar candy which was consumed by several eyewitnesses. If sugar candy seems like a strange thing to produce, it is important to remember that materializing wet and sticky substances is much harder to fake than dry powder. The American and Icelandic professors who investigated Baba's ability to materialize substances were convinced that their criteria for genuineness had not been breached. One of them concluded, 'Nowhere have I found phenomena which points so clearly and forcibly to spiritual reality.'

The third kind of miracle appears to be psychosomatic, involving the mind, body and the bridging emotions. One of the most dramatic examples of this is in the cure of John Gilbert, a chronic American invalid with no hope of outliving his afflictions. Then, by chance, he witnessed a drowned child being brought back to life and the wonder of this compassionate rescue altered his negative assessment of his own chances to live. Thankfulness for the gift of life banished the self-pity that had crippled his mind along with his wasted body. The case of Sai Baba bringing Walter Cowan back from the dead is another instance of miraculous intervention. Its significance lies not in the physical extension given to Cowan (he only lived for another eighteen months) but in Sai Baba's motive. He did it purely as a practical gesture to save the aged wife the added burden of taking her husband's body back to America. Almost all the miracles when subjected to scrutiny will reveal some compassionate motivation. There is a clue here to what motivates a miracle. Sathya Sai does not offer, for example, a cure for baldness. His concern is to enrich the inner rather than the outer man.

Though he calls his miracles 'presents for my family', they are spontaneous sparks from his divine nature. In an article entitled 'The Greater Miracle', Kamaladevi Chattopadhyay the doyenne of Indian social workers, makes it clear that the real miracle lies in confronting Sathya Sai's boundless affection, 'a force that can hardly be described . . . the quickening of the divine spark within us'.

*

Miracles are a grace and they betray the mechanics of how grace works. I can cite one small act of grace that, in the event would save my life. When Sai Baba visited Rani-ma's Delhi house in 1980, she asked him to bless my ice-axe as I was leaving shortly for an expedition to the Nanda Devi Sanctuary. Baba took the axe, which had both a pick and a spoon, and producing vibhuti, rubbed it on the pick but not the spoon. 'You will be successful,' he said as he handed it back. While climbing the face of a sheer gorge wall without rope, I used the pick of the axe to try and find a hold. As the blade on which Baba had rubbed vibhuti went into the cliff face, I lost my foothold and was left dangling—with all my weight on the pick—300 feet above the Rishi Ganga. The pick held firm long enough for the porters to back down and rescue me.

Having been graced with mini-miracles, I never needed to be convinced of the larger miracles in the lives of others. However, there is one I cannot ignore since it lasted twenty-five years and I was witness to its unfolding. Rani-ma's mother, Balbir Kaur, had cancer of the stomach and was operated on by the best surgeon in Bombay who concluded that she would not live till the morning. She kept a photo of Baba in her room and prayed to him as only a dying person can. She did not know who he was and had been given the photo by a relative who assured her this person was a healer who worked miracles. That night her body stopped sloughing and to the astonishment of the doctor who expected to find her dead in the morning, she was found alive and recovering. Not only did she live but she went on to supervise the ladies section of the Puttaparthi ashram with the punishing hours that the work involved. Furthermore, she led from the front, providing physical labour along with her volunteers to help construct the Sarva Dharma Stupa. She was one of Sai Baba's many living miracles, cured by the mixture of her faith and his love. The rationalists argue that it was the medicine that cured her despite the fact that the doctors had stopped giving her medicine because of its futility. They also argue that, technically, her cancer may not have been cured, but the fact remains she was restored to twenty-five years of vigorous activity.

The lengthy list of miracles that have marked Sathya

Sai's career can be found in any of the dozen books chronicling his disciples' experiences of such phenomena. Howard Murphet's *Sai Baba: Man of Miracles* (1971) gives a more objective account than Kasturi's official biography. An earlier list was compiled by Nagamani Purnaiya (*The Divine Leelas of Bhagavan Sri Sathya Sai Baba*) who was a very close disciple in the early days of the mission. Ra Ganapati includes a list of 370 miracles in the appendix to *Baba Satya Sai* and also gives an account of the strange swapping of Rani-ma's lingam by Baba. Erlendur Haraldsson's *Miracles Are My Visiting Cards: An Investigative Report on the Psychic Phenomena Associated with Sri Sathya Sai Baba* (1987) is a clinical account of a scholar's several meetings with Sathya Sai. While it is impartial in its observations, it is clear that Sathya Sai emerges from the study in a more favourable light than his accusers. Dr Narasimhaiah, who orchestrated the critics' cause, did rationalism a disservice by allowing his sincerity to be overcome by inquisitorial posturing.

Two miracles taken at random, which were witnessed by the same American scientist, show how the universal spirit—the essence of Sai—works its grace even when the physical frame of the Puttaparthi saint is not present where the miracle occurs. Al Drucker, a NASA aerospace engineer, recalls (*Golden Age*, 1980) how, when flying a small plane low on fuel in an electric storm, he had been saved by a 'voice' coming on the radio that guided him safely back to land against seemingly insurmountable odds. To add to the mystery, ground control had no knowledge of this radio exchange. After repairs, the plane flew on to Mexico where, quite by chance, the pilot visited an ashram run by a devotee of Sathya Sai. The moment the pilot saw the latter's photograph he was convinced this was the 'voice' that had guided him to safety. Curiously, another American devotee, Charles Penn, had a strikingly similar experience in an aircraft buffeted by storm clouds. This episode would likewise direct his feet to Puttaparthi.

A second miracle of a completely different order occurred in 1975 at Prasanthi Nilayam, where Al Drucker had gone to offer his thanks to the voice that had saved his life. He took a photo of Sathya Sai (from a distance) walking in front of the ashram temple a few minutes after he had taken a close-up portrait of Sai Baba's profile. These two photographs comprise the front and back plates of Sai Baba's *Discourses on the Bhagavad Gita* (edited by Al Drucker, 1988). Look closely at the back cover and, uncannily, there is, perfectly placed and 'infra-imposed', a looming background facial image of Sathya Sai that has the numinous feel of a cosmic presence. Critics will call this a trick double-exposure, ignoring the physical reality that the only power who could fake so convincingly must be God himself.

Ultimately neither of these miracles adds to our understanding of Sathya Sai's strange powers. They were given to Al Drucker for his instruction and are quoted because they are typical of the experiences of hundreds of other enquirers. The first miracle happened because of a matter of life and death and shook the whole being, while the second only whetted the soul's appetite for knowing the wonder which underlies the fabric of the universe. Taken together they illustrate how a teacher can dog the footsteps of a likely devotee and, having hooked him by drastic intervention, thereafter uses lesser miracles like

222 Sri Sathya Sai Baba

the two-in-one photograph to give sporting evidence of the teacher's ongoing leela or divine play. What we do know is that the main miracle, to which the others are pointing, is to bring about the transformation of a human being from a state of mindless animal behaviour to an awareness of one's divine inheritance. When Hislop heard that Sathya Sai could perform the ultimate miracle of transforming human nature, he caught the next plane to India.

{15}

Scattering the Proud in Heart

The manifesto of the rationalist movement is to denigrate the world of the spirit and pour scorn on its miraculous aspects on the assumption that all supraphysical phenomena offend the laws of nature and can only be indulged in by frauds eager to capitalize on the credulity of the poor. That no attempt is made to separate genuine spiritual manifestation from the bogus variety suggests that the critics are not interested in the truth but in their preconceived version of the truth. Shirdi Sai would liken his critics to thirsty men who come to a tap with their pots held upside down and then complain there is no water.

No one can deny that superstition and obscurantism is often rightly equated with popular religion which for centuries has played on the gullibility of the illiterate. At great pilgrim gatherings the priests cleverly orchestrate seemingly divine interventions to impress the faithful and, by these means, guarantee an even greater congregation next year. So, at Sabarimala in Kerala, Ayyappa pilgrims would be thrilled by a supposedly divine fireworks display at the climax of the visit. Similarly on a fixed day, annually, the Kaveri at her source would overflow her sacred tank and the goddess would be credited for the priestly ingenuity that caused the inundation. No one blames the critics for exposing the blatant manipulation of human minds by avaricious temple authorities.

Thanks to the Dravidian leader, Periyar, who was outspokenly critical of the brahminical system, rationalism has a broader base in the south than in the north. A leading rationalist of the south was Abraham Kovoor who made it his life's mission to expose the fraud of holy men by examining in slow motion how they performed magician's tricks that seemed miraculous to an uncritical audience. His sincerity cannot be doubted and his exposure undoubtedly helped cut down the numbers of imposters who had hoped to harness blind belief to their trickery. Obviously, Kovoor welcomed publicity and went to the extent of offering big cash awards to any godman who could successfully perform a miracle to the satisfaction of the critics. When no one succeeded in winning the prize, Kovoor concluded his case had been won. There was no such thing as a miracle.

The crude and insensitive approach of this sort of investigation reminds us of the atheist Charles Bradlaugh who would flourish a stopwatch before his British audience and loudly challenge the Almighty to strike him dead 'within the next five minutes'. After the time elapsed and Mr Bradlaugh was seen to be still alive, the audience was supposed to conclude that God did not exist. But what if God had concluded from his compassion that Mr Bradlaugh, though a fool, did not merit the death penalty? What if God concluded that by allowing Mr Bradlaugh to live his allotted lifespan, perhaps some wisdom might penetrate his arrogant skull? Ironically, his comrade-in-arms Annie Besant did go on to embrace the spiritual life.

The most glaring shortcoming of the rationalist is his habit of leaving love out of the equation. Their approach is cerebral and misses out on ordinary human emotions. The rationalists use Sai Baba to attack what is in fact their main enemy—the freedom to cherish the world of the spirit. Reading the abuse they heap on the Puttaparthi teacher, it seems that they are not so much incensed against him as at the poor who flock to his gatherings. Their claim to act in the interest of the common man sounds hollow when they display so much contempt for the villager's preferences. An epitaph erected by grieving parents at the Kohima war cemetery catches the poignancy these critics fail to comprehend:

> To the world our Tom was just a soldier
> To us he was the whole world

*

Besides the rationalist critics there are those who can be called irrationalist. These follow a well-known pattern in the history of religion where an overenthusiastic disciple turns apostate and, in a bewildering reversal of emotions, denounces as Satan the very person he had the day before declared to be God. The best example of this neurotic behaviour is St. Paul who started his career as an enthusiastic Jewish persecutor of Christians. (It is an irony that the first Christian missionary gave his church its first martyr when Paul had St. Stephen stoned to death.) There is a discernible pattern in the behaviour of the Puttaparthi malcontents. First the guru builds them up, gives them a front-row seat to make them feel they are part of the ashram inner circle and generally showers attention in their direction. Then, assured of their love, the guru starts the work of demolishing their unreal self. They are now ignored, made to sit at the back and generally cut to size. The easy way out is for them to look for another guru who may be more responsive to the sensitivity of their souls. Alternatively, the indignant disciple writes a book damning the guru for his blindness in not recognizing the spiritual gold that lay concealed in the rejected ego.

I can sympathize with those who throw in the towel since I nearly did so myself on receiving the guru's brush-off treatment. Ultimately we have to find the teaching in our self and understand that the guru is only an outer representative of that which is undying within. Whether we latch on to this teaching by grace or effort, its truth liberates us from the ego's need to be always in the front row. Find the teacher within and it makes no difference where you sit. Nor will you need to write a book justifying how you were deceived by Sai Baba which left you no choice but to pour out your soul in overdone malice.

Tal Brooke was one such enthusiastic follower who became disenchanted with Sai Baba and wrote *Lord of the Air*. The book catches the flavour of those flower-power years when hundreds of idealistic young foreigners went around the East, sampling sects and cults like honeybees, gaining spiritual insights (according to them) wherever they went but never finding an ashram worthy of their souls to drop anchor at permanently. It is customary to find in these inexperienced travellers' tales claims of 'revealing' to the world what charlatans exist behind a guru's robes. Since they themselves appear to be charlatans by pretending to understand the meaning of teachings only experience can give, how could they hope to perceive a genuine teacher? (Gurdjieff once remarked to the intellectual Ouspensky that if the latter understood a fraction of the teachings he had written about in his books, Gurdjieff would touch his feet.)

Another disenchanted western devotee David Bailey, a musician from Britain, later used the Internet to try and discredit Sai Baba and his movement. Both Brooke and Bailey allege improper conduct but do not produce any evidence other than hearsay from other disgruntled disciples, many of whom hide behind a pseudonym on Bailey's web site. Brooke relies on an unidentified Anglo-Indian boy, who, being a poor Christian, could be a paid informer of the missionary lobby. (One paperback edition of *Lord of the Air* bears a missionary imprint.) As Whitefield's young Anglo-Indians have no occasion to frequent the ashram, this boy must have gone to hobnob with the foreigners. The ashram rules—which Brooke breaches—caution devotees (with an almost prophetic insight in this instance): 'Do not consort with strangers. They are likely to have ulterior motives, leading ultimately to unpleasantness.'

Bailey's whole case self-destructs when, recognizing his inability to discredit Sai Baba's reputation by salacious innuendo, he launches into a general tirade, farcical in the wildness of its allegations, against the ashram and its workings: Sai Baba's vibhuti, he asserts, is prepared in capsule form to dupe the public. But even allowing for the possibility that Bailey is the only discerning witness among half a million fools, how does it explain the copious outpouring of vibhuti at Shivaratri before huge crowds, all of whom cannot be as stupid as he implies. The orchestrated malice of his fulminations sound as overdone as a Victorian missionary's denunciation of the heathen. Both Brooke and Bailey revealingly revert to the vocabulary of the evangelist, accusing their target of having supped with the devil. This is quite common among innocents abroad and I recall the visit of a famous British Catholic monk, in Mirtola, whose first impressions of the temple arati ceremony convinced him he was in Hell, listening to (and recognizing) the rites of Satan. What is amusing in all these foreign reactions to culture shock is the implication that the visitors have a close working knowledge of the devil's tastes!

Like the stray rationalist voices, what these isolated critics are really saying is that they are the only reliable witnesses and that Sai Baba's thirty million followers are all simpletons. Such overkill reveals the familiar scenario of an unbalanced believer who, unsure of his moorings, takes on a guru to bail him out of his confusion. Religious hatred is a sign of misguided energies and this may explain why followers who turn apostate invariably express their frustration through sexual innuendo.

Throughout history every religious teacher worth the name has been the target of some avenging group and the easiest way to cast doubt on a holy person's character is insinuate deviant sexual conduct. This is the price teachers pay for insisting on the celibate life, though it should be noted that even Gurdjieff, who had no sexual hang-ups, was targeted. Instead of being sympathetic to a guru who gives up the comforts of family life to teach mankind, and make allowance for his inevitable physical loneliness, society sanctimoniously criticizes any apparent deviance from the path of sacrifice. Christ was accused of consorting with drunkards and prostitutes and, like Ramakrishna Paramhansa, alleged to have homosexual proclivities.

We can also see in the case of Ramana Maharishi how the rumour-mongers operate, spreading malice to make innocence seem like guilt. A romantic and insistent young lady once proposed to Ramana. The young sannyasi courteously declined the offer of marriage. The unbalanced lady tragically took her life and the incident was suppressed, only to surface fifty years later. Now the plot had been twisted to make out that the saint was somehow responsible. Otherwise (ran the rumour), why should the incident have been hushed up in the first place? The ashram authorities were in a no-win situation. To wish away the event, from a theoretical point of view, was not ideal behaviour but it was practical given what Ramana was trying to embody. Why should a single tragic incident distract public attention from Ramana's long-standing example of unswerving devotion? True to pattern, this version was spread by a foreign disciple turned apostate.

Sex in any ashram situation is an explosive subject and where you have, as in Puttaparthi, thousands of devotees of the both genders sitting alongside one another twice daily for the ostensible purpose of darshan, it is small wonder that sometimes feelings spiral out of control. Where these are discreetly acknowledged, nothing is said, though it is strict ashram policy not to encourage liaisons for the obvious reason that the aim of coming to Puttaparthi is to get beyond physical desires. It is love of the universal spirit which is encouraged. Eros in such a setting is considered inappropriate though there can be a great flow of this powerful life force during darshan. Sai Baba has stated that the reason men and women should not converse unnecessarily on the campus is because it will distract them from the purpose for which they have come, namely to find their inner selves.

Unlike the famous contemporary guru Amritananda Mata who expresses her love by hugging everyone who comes for her darshan, Sathya Sai's strict distancing of himself from any human, and particularly female, touch is well vouched for. As with all holy figures who make a point of such segregation, vulgar rumour will ignore the practical precautions necessary in a mass gathering and assume that there must be some hidden homosexual preference. To silence such rumour is hard in a world where the priesthood of religions constrained by the vow of celibacy too often falls short of its proclaimed ideal. Hinduism is the only religion with the wisdom to perceive that sex must be a matter of taboo not because it is profane but because it is too sacred a mystery for idle talk.

Both Brooke and Bailey plead that their innocent belief had been abused by Sai Baba. By closing their eyes to the reality that every new disciple is fussed over and thereafter conspicuously dumped (for four years in the case of Diana Baskin and her husband), they have only themselves to blame. Sai Baba never invited either to Puttaparthi nor did he ask them to become his disciples. He did not promise them life after death if they made a contract with him to be their saviour. They came of their own free will. When he gave them importance they called him God. When he transferred that importance to others they called him Satan. Half a century of daily practice at Puttaparthi should have warned them of what to expect had they not shut their eyes to everything except their own self-importance. Bailey now admits he finds no need for external gurus which means that Sai Baba did manage to get one critical teaching across. Howard Murphet notes in his latest book that the fallout from these publications has had the salutary effect of purging Prasanthi Nilayam of other doubters, hangers-on and the merely curious.

*

A third category of critic can be called the literary dilettante who is intrigued by the mystique exuded by this guru figure but feels that anything populist must be avoided. They call themselves rationalist and humanist, but their lifestyle is far removed from the toils of the villager and they prefer to lecture the masses rather than mingle with them. These dedicated Sai Baba baiters display a fury out of all proportion to their otherwise gentle and enlightened outlook. Sathya Sai remarked about these 'hole-pickers' that their obsession with him, negatively at least, proves a subliminal concern for the divine. Like most urban critics, the dilettantes choose to ignore Baba's social achievements in providing drinking water for a thousand villages and continue to berate him for 'misleading' the poor.

Having grown up with a few of today's famous editors and watched them blossom into writers and persons of principle, I find it strange, if not funny, that these otherwise fair-minded professionals should, on being promoted to editorship, feel themselves competent to pronounce instant judgement on the character and mission of someone so profoundly mystifying as Sathya Sai. Mature editors will couch their indifference to the spiritual realm in considered prose but too often there is an irresponsible urge to make headlines and damn on hearsay since it is fashionable not to be seen as supporting anything that appeals to mass tastes. In one striking instance Sai Baba did neutralize the bad karma that press persons recklessly invite. R.K. Karanjia, the editor of India's then most populist and outspoken weekly, *Blitz*, who could be expected to pour scorn on Sai Baba's mission, was completely bowled over by Baba's presence and then went to the other extreme by claiming, 'God is an Indian.' There is a clue here as to why Sathya Sai's success has earned a bad press abroad. In all the adverse reports the common thread is phobia, a fear that Sai Baba's supernormal powers prove he is a bogeyman. To aggravate these often racist feelings of the international press is the economic reality that in the West, where church funds are declining, the newcomer Sai's mission is attracting high-profile donors. Envy at such spiritual success is another reason behind the critics' wanton downplaying of Sathya Sai's true spiritual status.

When a leading Indian weekly lifted wholesale a scurrilous and motivated anti-Sai Baba piece of propaganda from a London daily, it had to backtrack out of fear of a readership backlash. The anger was not about Sai Baba but Indian self-respect. Why should a magazine, without investigating the matter, reprint a planted India-baiting article? The newspaper in question is the mouthpiece of the Tory establishment, well known for its insular and colonialist outlook. Anything negative about the Hindu religious tradition is sure to be highlighted in its pages. It was this newspaper which raised a subscription for the cashiered General Dyer who ordered the shooting down of civilians at the Jallianwala Bagh massacre in 1919.

A prominent Indian daily, likewise, ran into heavy flak over the same story and had to issue an apology for upsetting its readership. Newspapers are not printed for the welfare of our soul but to make money for their owners. Since their proprietors have their own gurus, it is not surprising to find on occasion scurrilous reports on rival spiritual leaders.

A recent BBC documentary purporting to be an objective exposé of life in Puttaparthi ashram was in fact a propaganda exercise for the malcontents. Since its hostile agenda guaranteed that there would be no voicing of the ashram point of view, the BBC (ultimately answerable to the Church of England-inspired establishment) stooped to the unethical use of spy cameras.

*

One area where many well-wishers feel the Sathya Sai mission has been lacking is in the appointment of a public relations spokesperson with whom the press can interface. Often, resentment in the press is caused by the official ashram policy of remaining silent, which suggests (at least to the media) either an autocratic set-up or having something to hide. Thus, you have the canard put out by rival missions and taken up by the press that Puttaparthi is a sinister cult where the teacher practises a kind of hypnosis to silence his followers into blind obedience. This conveniently ignores the fact that the press can also behave high-handedly and is at pains to hide its potential for mischief. Once you engage with the media, there is no end to their demands. Anyone who has ever granted an interview has learnt to expect to find his words distorted and his views misrepresented. Damaging headlines that are proved false are apologized for in small print. The press, seeking ephemeral titillation, too often evades its responsibility to uphold everyday let alone eternal values.

A being with greater reserves of compassion, on entering the human body, has to accept both the severe scrutiny his message will attract and the guarantee that his body is susceptible to all the complaints that the flesh is heir to. As the fare provided by newspapers shows, most readers prefer scandal, violence and calamity to the arts of peace and the balm of the spirit. Sathya Sai has brought life to over a thousand thirsty villages in Rayalseema but no journalist will think it worth his while to spread the word about the historic dimensions of this unique act of charity. However, just one murder in the ashram will bring hordes of press persons keen to revive the mood of the ancient blood sport of throwing Christians to the lions.

When an internal ashram murder did rock Puttaparthi in 1993, Sathya Sai himself summed it up as the fruit of envy. However, this did not prevent the press from having a field day in wild speculation and inventive reporting. A study of the press clippings in the wake of this sensational case must make any professional journalist wince at the shoddy amateurism and cheap innuendo that emerges. If the ashram ever needed a case that it had been right to keep the press at bay, here was the best evidence for it. Some raw young reporter would turn up at the ashram campus, announce that the devotees were observing a 'conspiracy of silence' and then from this silence deduce the most ludicrous, unsubstantiated story.

Inevitably, the traumatic suddenness of the tragedy and the ensuing melee, when devotees with emotions at fever pitch gathered in confusion, guaranteed there would be conflicting versions of the sequence of events. It seems that four of Sai Baba's own security detail broke into his living quarters (attached to the temple) late at night. Armed with what looked like home-made knives, they murdered Baba's favourite aide and another student who came to his defence. The four then went upstairs apparently to confront Sai Baba to apprise him of their grievances, slashing everything in their way, but they fell back when Baba ordered them to go. By now the alarm had been raised since senior students were sleeping outside the temple. Baba was rescued by his students and lodged safely in a temple storeroom. Even as he sat on a bag of rice, someone remarked on how he had been betrayed by his own inner circle. Sathya Sai, pointing to the sack, said that only a few grains of rice were bad. At the height of the trauma he still had compassion for the killers.

The local police had been summoned in the meantime and climbed up to Sai Baba's quarters where the four murderers had locked themselves in. Sathya Sai had sounded off an alarm that had been fitted to warn the ashram of any Naxalite threat which had seemed imminent at one time. This aroused the villagers who came armed with sticks to swell the crowd of devotees whose mood had turned volatile on hearing that Sathya Sai was under siege. Not known for their sophisticated response to delicate situations, the local police did what most local police anywhere in India would do—they opened fire on the attackers. A panel of the door behind which they had been hiding had been knocked out by rifle butt and, according to the police, they fired in self-defence after the murderers came at them with knives. All four were killed. Two of the conspirators got away on a motorbike and these (who were later apprehended) are thought to be the masterminds behind the attack. However, Sai Baba never brought charges against them and the case lapsed. The press read something sinister in the avoidance of a long-drawn-out legal remedy, overlooking Sathya Sai's prime concern that the families of those involved (most of whom are his devotees) should not be further afflicted.

The word 'conspiracy' is a great favourite with the press, offering unlimited scope for speculation. This was given further prominence when it was claimed that some landmines and poisonous chemicals were found in the room of one of the absconders. (But if there had been a conspiracy to sabotage the ashram why did the assailants resort to hand-made knives?) Nowhere in the press clippings is the simplest of motives considered—jealousy of Radhakrishnan, Baba's aide who was stabbed so violently that it suggests the pent-up hatred of a typical medieval Deccan court, where a usurper would backstab a rival who had taken his place in the sultan's favour. In fact, there probably was a romantic angle to the crime. It seems the aide had fallen in love with a woman and Sathya Sai is believed not to have approved of the match. The murderers were jealous of the aide's closeness to

Baba and further incensed when he refused to give up the woman. The press was more enamoured of a conspiracy at the national level. A leader of the minority-baiting Vishwa Hindu Parishad was a regular visitor to the ashram and one of the conspirators had recently attended a VHP meeting in Bangalore. As if to balance this communal theory, the name of a Muslim from the Bombay underworld was floated as seeking to assassinate Puttaparthi's prominent saint.

Yet another slant given by the press was of infighting between ashram factions for control of the considerable assets that have accrued to Sathya Sai. Concocted stories of strange goings-on and of mafia activities may have tickled the readership but hardly made sense to anyone who knows Puttaparthi. The young reporters exaggerated the situation manifold. When, by their own admission, no one in the ashram would talk to them, it follows that much of what they wrote was inspired hearsay. The ashram was in a no-win situation since the press arrived with a hostile agenda.

*

To swell the chorus of these abrasive critics, who saw it as their life's mission to humiliate Sathya Sai and find under his fairy prince image an ugly frog, was Dr Narasimhaiah, the head of a rationalist organization supposedly humane in its instincts yet impudent in its demands that any free citizen should submit himself unreservedly to its self-styled committee for scrutiny. As the vice chancellor of Bangalore University, Dr Narasimhaiah may have thought that the dignity of his

office would lend support to his witch-hunt in the name
of encouraging the scientific temper. In fact, the VC used
the imposition of Mrs Gandhi's Emergency (which
curtailed democratic rights and encouraged petty tyrants)
to set up a handpicked committee which, with maximum
press publicity, drove in two buses to the Whitefield
ashram and demanded that Baba appear and be
interviewed by them. The objective of the outing appears
to have been no more than creating a public spectacle.
The rationalists seemed to bask more in their self-
importance than in wishing seriously to examine Sathya
Sai's psychic phenomena. Otherwise, they would have
adopted a more conciliatory approach. When Sai Baba
declined to indulge the whim of the delegation, to the
VC's chagrin, instead of depleting the numbers who went
to Sai Baba, public sympathy led to an increase. As if to
rub salt in his rationalist wounds, the vice chancellors
who followed him happened to be Sai devotees. When
Sathya Sai started his own university at Puttaparthi, the
chancellor naturally was Sathya Sai himself. Within a
decade, this institution for higher learning has become
one of India's leading universities. There is something
profoundly symbolic in the different ways these two
figures have approached life's mysteries. Dr Narasimhaiah,
as an earnest intellectual, reached the pinnacle of academic
achievement, yet due to his singularly graceless lack of
regard for those who did not share his crusading zeal, he
failed to move his fellow men. By contrast, the half-
educated villager Sathya Sai won over the world with his
greater depth of understanding. In addressing the needs
of the heart he demonstrated that most people can
distinguish between fine-sounding words and inborn
wisdom.

Sathya Sai's willingness to discuss the mystery of his nature with those sympathetic to the subject is well known. On several occasions Sai Baba has expressed his willingness to put his powers under scrutiny, but only if the motive is not to denigrate the divine. As has been seen, where psychic investigators are serious and objective, Sai Baba has been happy to cooperate in their controlled experiments. Two foreign academics and other serious students of the psychic realm have, in fact, written a treatise on the subject but, being of a positive nature, such findings do not lend themselves to journalistic sensationalism.

The critics spoil their case by prejudging the issue of the genuineness of Sathya Sai's miracles. They do not set out to enquire objectively but to debunk. Their hostility appears to derive from some kind of phobia. After news of the ashram murder, Dr Narasimhaiah gloatingly reported that Baba instead of using his divine powers to turn the four murderers into frogs 'did exactly what I would do and ran away'. Of course, if Baba had in fact used any special siddhi to incapacitate the attackers he would then be charged with performing an inhuman and unlawful act.

It is interesting to observe the rationalist's opinion of his own worth and the question arises as to why these people, with so much to teach mankind, spend time seeking to expose fraud in others. Surely, the simplest way to prove Sai Baba's limitations is for critics like Dr Narasimhaiah to exceed Baba's charitable works with their own. When they attract thirty million of their fellow men to their message they have every right to demand that the world take them more seriously.

Writing books against Sai Baba or seeking to tarnish his reputation on the Internet might merit an audience if the authors of these grievances possessed some locus standi in the world of philanthropy. If they had done a thousandth part of what Sathya Sai has accomplished in furthering the welfare of humanity, we would be justified in taking their complaints seriously and consider investigating whether pure water can flow from a polluted spring. The critics belong to the category of intellectuals who cannot face the reality of the spirit and desperately want to explain it away. They are haunted by the truth Sathya Sai embodies and wish to negate a presence that millions of ordinary people regard as the most beautiful evidence they have of life's ultimate meaning. What is common to all the critics is a boundless contempt for the affections of the common citizen in his or her choice of religious expression. It is to heal these perverse perceptions that the masters of all faiths have arrived amongst us. Sai Baba's reply to the critics is that whatever miracles happen are not due to his human form but because of compassion and love that have made it their tool.

Epilogue

I know there were two religions among the ancients—
for the vulgar and the learned—but I think one love
might have served both of them very well.

—Laurence Sterne in
Tristram Shandy

The twenty-first century promises to see an Asian resurgence wherein India's role, as always, will be of a guiding spirit, reaffirming values based on the human soul's direct awareness of life's undying mystery. For centuries, Hindu dharma has been doctored and diluted to suit a supposed spiritual elite and the present study suggests that the Sai Parampara offers a corrective remedy, answering the need of modern India's vibrant democracy. It directs us to realize the divine being within, rather than cultivate external intermediaries, brahminical or otherwise.

In my forty years of travel around the subcontinent, viewing the changing religious landscape, I find the most remarkable feature has been the 'fixed star' status of Sai Baba whether in Shirdi or Puttaparthi. Dozens of gurus

have come and gone, displaying a flicker or two of the
spirit, but in none save Sai Baba have I encountered the
light of the unwavering love that sustains and gives
meaning to existence. Of course, others will have their
own valid experiences of different paths and teachers, but
for this particular student the Sai aura is the greatest
wonder discovered on his voyage East. Devotees tend to
ignore the repeated assertion of Sathya Sai that he has
come to win over the non-devotee. This is why the Sai
Parampara appeals to a non-believer (in the outer forms)
like myself since it dispenses with the hysteria, cant and
humbug customarily associated with religion and delivers,
not sermons, but skills anyone can harness to his search
for reality.

Sathya Sai possesses easily the most charismatic of
presences I have experienced, electrifying in the crackle of
the supercharged energy he gives off. My heart
spontaneously responds to his divine aura. Added to this
is the knowledge that comes across, that true religion is
about living and has little to do with the trappings of
conventional religiosity. Sathya Sai, despite my serious
reservations about anyone who parades his or her beliefs
in holy cloth, has the ability to arouse in me the
profoundest love and move my soul so deeply that all
mental questioning is stilled. (Well, nearly all.) I have no
idea whether he is God or man—or both—but this
doesn't affect his impact on my soul in the slightest. I
know what I feel and that buoyant reality is beyond
verbal definition. I feel indescribably graced that I was
born to see an aspect of divinity that has not been
witnessed on earth for thousands of years.

Because of its fiery nature, love is a desperate remedy

resorted to by those who are passionate about finding who they are and why they are here. The limitation many Sai devotees impose on their understanding is to confine love to their particular parish, Shirdi or Puttaparthi. The danger with internalizing the Sai teaching is for the devotee to feel that the goal has been attained when his soul is attuned to the divine. But the real work is to realize Schiller's *Alle menschen wirden bruder*, and regard the whole world as one undivided family. The message of both saints is that their essence—the divine grace of love—outlives the body. Whatever or whomsoever we love releases a grace that takes us closer to the divine.

According to the Koran, 'Allah will give of his bounty to every man of grace,' and the impact of two uncommon citizens of the Deccan on an ordinary traveller's life amply bears out the truth of this. My aim has been to try and view the receiving end of divine grace, and how, as Ezra Pound exquisitely puts it, 'the light doth melt us'. This study of the working of grace in the Deccan tells the marvellous story of inner wealth and outer poverty, brutal environmental challenge and tender human response. According to current civilizational theory, Anantapur district should be the last place on the map to display any visible signs of human happiness and for that we should look to London or New York. Yet, people from all over the world flock to Puttaparthi where Sai Baba's presence stands worldly logic on its head. The theorists forgot to factor in the desperate need of the human soul to experience love.

As a teenager I went to Glasgow to hear a much-touted evangelist of the American evangelical persuasion. The atmosphere I experienced suggested an unhealthy,

neurotic manipulation of the audience's guilt complex.
Alistair Cooke, the famous broadcasting journalist, has
written an exposé of how fundamentalist preachers (of all
religions) use the same technique of whipping up mass
sentiment as a means to loosen our rational faculty and
make us susceptible to their blandishments which range
from appeals to donate one's soul to one's bank balance.
This latter attempt 'to render unto God what is Caesar's'
contrasts vividly with the mood I have come to associate
with Sathya Sai.

The grace I feel at Puttaparthi when I behold Sai Baba
is wholesomely world-affirming, almost like being at a
wedding, where the atmosphere is both sensuous and
spiritual, being and body dovetailed by the magical aura
of love. This mood is caught in a traditional Celtic
prayer:

Those who reject the power of love
Are like a leaking ship on a stormy sea
Or an apple tree that never blossoms.
Those who attend the call of love
Are like a chalice overflowing with wine
Or a beautiful bride awaiting her groom.

My travels from West to East (the proper direction for
acquiring wisdom if East stands for the inner witness)
proved nothing that I did not know before I started. Yet,
without that journey, my certainty in the oneness of
religion would have remained of the frail intellectual
variety. To experience that feeling of oneness is the real
proof, for only then does all argument fall silent. Ramana
Maharishi tells the story of a merchant who went all the
way round the globe in search of a rare jewel. It was only

when he came back home did he, looking in a mirror, discover it resting upon his own forehead. The saint emphasized that without the arduous and seemingly futile journey, the seeker would never have found the treasure he sought. In other words, he had learnt the hard way that looking in a mirror can be more than a statement of vanity.

My friends, when told I was writing a book on Sai Baba, quite justifiably from their point of view (that sees the Sai Parampara as a kind of curiosity to be noted in passing), expressed surprise and asked, 'What do you know about Sathya Sai Baba?' I confess I know very little but I write of him because on every occasion I have seen him I experience the heart-warming feeling that this man—and here millions round the world will agree—reflects a truth I know to be the real me. So this book is not really about Sai Baba at all but about the elated feeling he arouses in me and others, the love my heart cherishes as the only thing worth having in the universe. It is satisfying for someone who has had a long and often precarious innings to be able to pen his gratitude to a person for confirming his profoundest feelings about life (before he departs to another level). I do not have any outwardly intimate connection with Sai Baba and yet he has been a presiding grace, hovering above the writing of this book when I felt the project was beyond me. This seems to strengthen the argument that Sai Baba's main appeal is to backsliders and 'pseudo-dons'!

There is also the secondary pleasure of completing a cycle, since my first book *Seven Sacred Rivers* began with the observation, 'the important thing, whether one travels the globe or journeys within is to find love'. While on a high Himalayan trek, I camped above the tree line in a log cabin facing the mighty peak of Shiva's Trisul. This unlikely spot seemed to have been chosen for a honeymooners' tryst since freshly and boldly carved into its planks were the words 'Love is energy beyond the power of thought'. How extraordinary to find so far from mortal trafficking such an unexpected reaffirmation by unknown hands of the inner wisdom experienced by the human heart. It is at moments like this, when grace seems to overwhelm with its attentions, that the effort of toiling along the mountain path seems so supremely worthwhile.

*

In matters of the spirit, unless you have experienced something of the subject, most discussion remains academic and can be ludicrously at odds with the inner facts. Cricket's most literary luminary, Neville Cardus, has cautioned any would-be writer not to write unless inwardly compelled to do so, and never to write about anything you have not experienced. We are all taught to believe that death is a sinister subject, especially when it stalks the body of one who is young. At the age of twenty-six, I almost died of typhoid. For forty days I fasted (on a liquid diet) and, instead of being mortified at the prospect of a dolorous transition, my soul was filled with a beatific rapture of orgiastic dimensions. While it lasted, my whole being seemed to pour forth the poetry of thankfulness at the wonder of creation. There was no way death could rob me of this glorious reality, a universal spirit whose great engine I could hear as a rhythmic background throb. What could—and did—rob me was my own body. The moment I started eating, the rapture faded. This eye-opening encounter with the reality of the spirit totally changed the way I looked at things and forced me to accept that almost all the notions about life I had inherited were based on hearsay, not experience. As Joseph Campbell would have put it, my youth had been spent in painstakingly climbing a ladder placed against the wrong wall! Since then, my ears attune themselves not to what a person says, but gauges whether he has experienced what he is describing. The great body of Sai Parampara followers, I imagine, use the same touchstone. They are unconcerned about what the rationalists or orthodox may say because they have found what their soul had been looking for.

In a sense, it is irrelevant whether Sai Baba is God, avatar or saviour. These are all projections of the spirit within. That spirit is not a projection nor is it a lifeless projector. As Orage, the Gurdjieffian, reminds us: 'You are the pianist not the piano.' More than figuring out Sathya Sai's status it is important to know and appreciate his ability to arouse the divine in anyone who sincerely seeks this grace. One who can do that, whether you call him a fakir or a magician, deserves serious respect. His presence alone reaffirms your soul's immaculacy, clearing the clouds your mind had caused to gather over it. To those who wonder how an avatar can play table tennis, win sack races, go on picnics, build a planetarium and cricket stadium in his village or open a Marks and Spencer type store for his devotees, the answer is that love makes its own rules.

What absurd confidence tricks religious doctrine plays

on mankind! How fatuous is the notion of sin when we behold the undying effulgence of that inner reality. (The historian Romila Thapar has made the profound observation that the continuity of India's wisdom is due to the absence of Satan in her culture.) We and our bright ideas do not run the universe. Nor does it run as a loveless mechanism. It is powered by the irresistible force that Sathya Sai personifies and whose message is plain:

> *There is only one religion,*
> *the religion of love.*
> *There is only one caste,*
> *the caste of humanity.*
> *There is only one language,*
> *the language of the heart.*

As the man on the street—irrespective of his faith—knows, it is love that makes the world go round. Sathya Sai is the soul's guide who teaches us how to shrug off our limited notions and understand that we are at one with that love, our immortal essence. Luther, the reforming monotheist, would reaffirm, 'Love is the living essence of the divine nature.'

We can forget, if need be, the outer Sai and all the trappings of religion, since they can only be imitations of the one real thing. They will pass—unlike the power of love they briefly embody. As the Sai Parampara shows, that 'thing' we call love can come in the garb of an irascible fakir, a graceful incarnation of love or a (yet to be) saint who will strive to unify mankind. Those who travel to Puttaparthi or Shirdi or Gunaparthi (in the future) will find little unless they go with love in their hearts. How can we find meaning in Sai Baba if we have lost it in ourselves? Religion has betrayed the common man's trust by imposing elitist hierarchies in the name of God. The Deccan saints are sons of the soil who trust not only the love of God, but that of their fellow men in whatever guise it may appear.

In India, the custom of offering namaste, reverencing the divine in the other person, has a profound meaning which daily usage has all but killed. We do not bow because the other is more senior, rich or important but because, deep within, we recognize that the human form contains the great mystery of selfhood. We are in fact bowing to a reflection of ourselves. In a letter written to Rajagopal (published in Diana Baskin's book), Baba concludes with—and underlines the words—'*You are Sai*'. It is the truth of this formula which our lives should be testing, but as Diana notes, 'The energy we waste in criticizing others is just what is needed to make us live up to our own ideals.'

The critics who rail against the daily spiritual theatre enacted at Puttaparthi may technically be only half-wrong. Everything outside us, to that extent, is phony since it is but a reflection of the real within. Sathya Sai would be the first to agree that what he appears to be is something quite different from what he actually is. One glaring fact the critics overlook is that it is they who are obsessed with the outer image of Sai Baba and not the devotee who exults in finding him seated in his own heart. All true devotees insist they go to Shirdi and Puttaparthi to charge their batteries. They recognize that the source of the spirit is hidden in the mystery of one person's—everyman's—selfhood. The ultimate theological significance of the Sai Parampara is in this daring

relocation of divinity from place to person. We can
explore that self in our own homes as well as travel to
Puttaparthi to see it uniquely enshrined in a human body.
To witness such grace is well worth the effort the journey
involves, but the real Puttaparthi, the City of God on the
Philosopher's Mount, will prove even more wonderful,
once you find the way.

It makes little difference whether you are rich or poor
when travelling that path. What is important is the
realization that all mortals have the capacity to father or
mother forth sons, outer *and* inner. The whole point
about why we have children is to enable them to find
what we have been seeking. Sex is not the demon that
conventional religion makes it out to be, it is the divine
urge giving us a hint in physical bliss of where the divine
child resides. It is up to us to accept that the most
ordinary of parents—like Venkappa Raju and
Easwaramma—can be the vehicle for the incarnation of
love's divine offspring. Each one of us is Venkappa Raju
and Easwaramma—awaiting our inner self to be born as
Sathya Sai. He is the short answer to the question of who
we really are. This he does by showing us what we are
not, which in turn reveals the potential of what we can
become.

In his presence you may not recognize the
undifferentiated atman nor necessarily feel the gravitas
that goes with beholding God. You may not even relate
positively to Sai Baba's slight form. What you do register
though is the ineffable realization that, thanks to this
diminutive person's abounding grace, you are face to face
with the miracle of love. And this you know for certain
to be a reflection of your own real self. Rani-ma, who

understands the limitations of words and has no need of
the crutch of logic, seems to have got it right when she
keeps reminding me: 'I don't believe Sai Baba is God.
He's something much *more*.'

That just about sums up my experience of being in
love.

*

A man's life, if he approaches seventy years, consists of
some 25,000 days and for most of us these are devoted
almost entirely to our own convenience. With Sathya Sai,
not only the days but the nights have been dedicated
without fail to furthering the welfare of his devotees. It
is in the accumulation of such applied virtue that his
miraculous nature is best seen. The uninterrupted concern
for his devotees is another link with Shirdi Baba who
went as far as to say he was a slave to his disciples,
averring that 'night and day I think of my people'. He
viewed them as orphaned children and they in turn felt
themselves to be a part of his Sai family.

Whereas orthodox religion binds its followers with
the adhesives of fear and conformity, the Sai Parampara
flourishes on the vital bond that unites teacher and pupil.
The contrast is best seen between the mood that affects
a congregation to be visited by a high ecclesiastical
personage or a famous preacher, and the way villagers
and devotees of Puttaparthi react to the news of the
return of their Baba. The first will be formally correct
and accompanied by the appropriate ceremonial whereas
the latter is aquiver with the anticipation of the return of
the prodigy. News of his car being sighted brings the

populace out in a rush. The gopuram gate, kept closed in the absence of Bhagavan, is hastily swung open, and devotees spontaneously line up with conch shells to serenade the arrival of the bridegroom. What was a dead campus sparks into a living body. Here is resurrection with a vengeance, the miracle of grace streaming forth before your eyes as the coordinates of love and longing meet and merge.

Index

258   Index